T0293632

Advanced Research on Asian Economy and Economies of Other Continents – Vol. 10

Economic Dynamism, Openness, and Inclusion

How Singapore Can Make the Transition from an Era of Catch-up Growth to Life in a Mature Economy

Advanced Research on Asian Economy and Economies of Other Continents
(ISSN: 1793-0944)

Series Editor: HOON Hian Teck
(Singapore Management University, Singapore)

The escape from the Malthusian trap dating from the Industrial Revolution in the eighteenth century began in Europe and its North American offshoots and spread to different parts of the world. Technological diffusion from these frontier economies enabled Japan, then the East Asian economies of Hong Kong, Singapore, South Korea and Taiwan and, somewhat later, China and India to experience catch-up growth. Yet, there are signs that the pace of innovation that propelled the engine of growth in the frontier economies has slowed down. The growth slowdown has been accompanied by widening income disparities and weaker labour market performance. What are the economic and non-economic forces that are likely to shape the evolution of the global economy in the twenty-first century? What type of institutions and policy measures would reinvigorate economic dynamism and bring about economic inclusion? With the end of catch-up growth, what are the challenges and opportunities facing Singapore and the other East Asian economies?

Published

Vol. 10   *Economic Dynamism, Openness, and Inclusion: How Singapore Can Make the Transition from an Era of Catch-up Growth to Life in a Mature Economy*
by Hian Teck Hoon (Singapore Management University, Singapore)

Vol. 9   *Economic Development of Taiwan: Early Experiences and the Pacific Trade Triangle*
by Frank S. T. Hsiao (University of Colorado, Boulder, USA) &
Mei-Chu Wang Hsiao (University of Colorado, Denver, USA)

Vol. 8   *Resilient States from a Comparative Regional Perspective:
Central and Eastern Europe and Southeast Asia*
by Bafoil François (Sciences Po Paris, France)

Vol. 7   *EU-Asia and the Re-Polarization of the Global Economic Arena*
edited by Lars Oxelheim (Lund University, Sweden & Research Institute of Industrial Economics, Sweden)

Vol. 6   *Asean Economic Integration: Trade, Foreign Direct Investment, and Finance*
by Michael G. Plummer (Johns Hopkins University, SAIS-Bologna, and East-West Center, Italy)

More information on this series can also be found at http://www.worldscientific.com/series/araeeoc

Advanced Research on Asian Economy and Economies of Other Continents – Vol. 10

Economic Dynamism, Openness, and Inclusion

How Singapore Can Make the Transition from an Era
of Catch-up Growth to Life in a Mature Economy

Hian Teck Hoon

Singapore Management University, Singapore

World Scientific

NEW JERSEY · LONDON · SINGAPORE · BEIJING · SHANGHAI · HONG KONG · TAIPEI · CHENNAI · TOKYO

Published by

World Scientific Publishing Co. Pte. Ltd.

5 Toh Tuck Link, Singapore 596224

USA office: 27 Warren Street, Suite 401-402, Hackensack, NJ 07601

UK office: 57 Shelton Street, Covent Garden, London WC2H 9HE

Library of Congress Cataloging-in-Publication Data
Names: Hoon, Hian Teck, author.
Title: Economic dynamism, openness, and inclusion : how Singapore can make the transition
    from an era of catch-up growth to life in a mature economy / Hian Teck Hoon.
Description: New Jersey : World Scientific, [2018] | Series: Advanced Research on Asian Economy
    and Economies of Other Continents ; volume 10 | Includes bibliographical references and index.
Identifiers: LCCN 2018001277 | ISBN 9789813236226
Subjects: LCSH: Economic development--Singapore. | Singapore--Economic policy. |
    Singapore--Economic conditions.
Classification: LCC HC445.8 .H675 2018 | DDC 330.95957--dc23
LC record available at https://lccn.loc.gov/2018001277

British Library Cataloguing-in-Publication Data
A catalogue record for this book is available from the British Library.

For any available supplementary material, please visit
http://www.worldscientific.com/worldscibooks/10.1142/10883#t=suppl

Desk Editor: Shreya Gopi

Typeset by Stallion Press
Email: enquiries@stallionpress.com

Printed in Singapore

Contents

Preface

It is not given to many countries to experience dramatic transformations that would lift an economy from relative poverty to high living standards all in the span of the last 50 years. Only a handful of countries have been able to achieve this, notably, the East Asian economies of Hong Kong, Singapore, South Korea, and Taiwan. The Singapore story, which is our focus in this book, is one of building secure property rights, a generally business-friendly environment, and a stable industrial relations climate that have encouraged a deep integration into the global economy. This combination of institution-building features enabled Singapore to launch into a phase of catch-up growth that has brought us from Third World to First World within a generation. Having been born in the year that Singapore gained self-government, I witnessed with my own eyes how catch-up growth, with its escalator-like movement, lifted up living standards with concomitant improvements in job opportunities and wage earnings for a large segment of the population.

High growth rates that characterised the catch-up phase, however, must give way to slower growth as Singapore becomes a mature economy. How slow is it likely to be? My aim in writing this book is to provide a coherent theory capable of explaining how we got to where we are so that we might use the same theory of growth to predict what the future might look like. The theoretical framework allows us to examine what policy choices we will have to make in order to achieve desired outomes in the face of new trade-offs. I emphasise the importance of establishing economic dynamism, economic openness, and economic inclusion in the next phase of Singapore's economic development.

I draw upon my training as an economist in writing this book. For example, I use the framework of economic growth and notions of the natural rate of unemployment in thinking about what determine Singapore's standard of living, employment, and wage earnings. Two teachers at Columbia University, Professors Ronald Findlay and Edmund Phelps, have been huge influences in my intellectual development. The role of international trade in shaping a country's economic performance came home to me from classes that I took with Professor Findlay. From Professor Phelps, with whom I've had many years of research collaboration, I learned how to think systematically about the general-equilibrium effects of economic shocks and policy on the long swings of economic activity. I owe a great debt to both of them. I would also like to express appreciation to my wife, Lian Leck, with whom I have discussed many of the ideas in this book.

About the Author

Hoon Hian Teck is Professor of Economics at the Singapore Management University. He specialises in macroeconomics, international trade, and economic growth. A major theme of his research focuses on understanding the big swings of economic activity — why nations experience slumps with elevated unemployment, for example — as well as business fluctuations. As a specialist also in trade, he has worked to embed trade effects on an endogenous natural rate of unemployment.

How Singapore managed to transit from Third World to First — as measured by GDP per capita — completing the process of convergence without being caught in the middle-income trap — and figuring out what is needed to generate economic prosperity as a mature economy has occupied his mind in recent years. His research examines the central role played by economic openness in explaining Singapore's catch-up growth and evolving income distribution. Since remaining integrated into the world economy brings both opportunities and threats, the question is how to structure institutions and policy to generate long-term gains across the whole of society while managing periodic external shocks.

Hian Teck is a past Vice-President of the Economic Society of Singapore (2002–2004) and he has served as a co-editor of the *Singapore Economic Review* since January 2002.

Introduction

Figure 0.1 plots Singapore's real Gross Domestic Product (GDP) per capita since 1900 along with the series for the United States (U.S.).[1] Before independence in 1965, Singapore's real GDP per capita was growing at a pace to just maintain its relative distance to the U.S. economy.[2] It then began to speed up to race towards the U.S. standard of living. Over the past 50 years, there has been a ten-fold increase in the standard of living for Singapore. Such an increase has been possible because the real GDP per capita has been growing, on average, at about five percent per annum over the past 50 years. Another way of putting it is to say that the standard of living has been doubling every 14 years. To see how remarkable a transformation can be made by maintaining a growth rate in real GDP per capita of five percent per annum, consider the experience of the U.S., the world economic leader in the 20th century. Since 1880, the U.S. economy has seen its real GDP per capita grow at an average annual rate of two percent per annum. At this rate, its standard of living has been doubling every 35 years; it, therefore, took the U.S. economy more than a century (115 years, to be precise) to see its living standard increase by a factor of 10. Singapore, however, took less than half the time that it has taken the U.S. economy to achieve a ten-fold increase in its standard of living. One reason

---

[1]The graph is plotted on a log scale so the slope of each line reflects the growth rate of real GDP per capita.

[2]Singapore was a British colony and attained self-government in 1959. In 1965, it became fully independent.

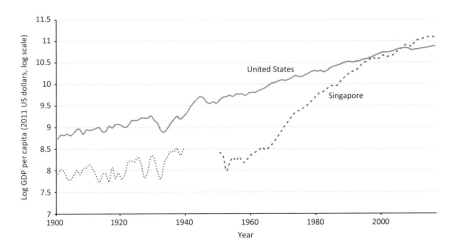

Figure 0.1:   Real GDP Per Capita in the United States and Singapore, 1900–2016

Source: Maddison Project Database, version 2018. Jutta Bolt, Robert Inklaar, Herman de Jong and Jan Luiten van Zanden, 2018, "Rebasing 'Maddison': New Income Comparisons and the Shape of Long-run Economic Development," Maddison Project Working Paper, nr.10.

Singapore could achieve this is that in its economic take-off it could copy the stock of technologies available in the world (rather than reinventing the wheel). The diffusion of technology from the world's technology leader enabled Singapore to launch into a process of catch-up growth.[3]

Given that the rise in the average person's standard of living is best described as a slow crawl from the perspective of the whole of human history, the transformation of Singapore from relative poverty as a British trading post to economic prosperity, all in a span of 50 years, is nothing short of extraordinary and is a tale worth telling. We are interested in understanding the mechanisms at work to achieve such a transformation since the income gap between rich and poor nations remains very huge. Why some countries are rich and others remain poor is a deeply important question that has major consequences for the welfare of millions of people in the world. Apart

---

[3]During the process of catch-up growth, the Singapore economy grows faster than the world's technology leader.

from possible lessons the Singapore story holds for others, it also remains very important to know what the economic possibilities are for the current and future citizens of Singapore, having now surpassed the U.S. standard of living as measured by real GDP per capita.[4] The approach in this book is not to provide a narrative of who did what, what worked, and what did not work. The first-generation leaders were remarkable people who saw beyond their own personal gains, faced huge obstacles, and made many sacrifices in order to make life better for their fellow countrymen. A careful study of their lives, how they came to be the sort of persons they were and made the choices they did, would be beneficial and inspiring for all of us. But that is not what this book sets out to do. Instead, its aim is to try to provide a theory of Singapore's economic development. With a coherent theory capable of explaining how we got to where we are, we might be able to use the same theory of growth to predict what the future might look like.

The book aims to develop a theoretical framework that will allow us to distil the economic (and non-economic) forces as well as the mechanisms they worked through to produce the lift from low living standards to economic prosperity. It seeks answers to questions such as: Having now reached the status of a rich country, what policy choices will we have to make in order to achieve desired outcomes in the face of new trade-offs? What predictions can we make about our economic future based on the framework we develop? In developing our framework, we go beyond the particular persons who lived in the particular historical times and made the particular decisions that affected their lives and those around them. We are interested more generally in private incentives, market forces, and their interaction with social influences and political institutions to bring about a historically unprecedented economic transformation in a relatively short span of time. We provide an analysis of how these same forces operate in a country that has completed the phase of catch-up growth and is now transiting to being a mature economy.

---

[4]The comparison of real GDP per capita is in purchasing power parity terms.

It is not just individual responses to incentives that affect an economy's productivity. Broad market forces also play a big part in driving living standards as well as shape the incentives that people face and determine aggregate outcomes at an economy-wide level. When appropriate laws and institutions were put in place to guide businesses, workers, and consumers in their decision making in an environment that was fully open to the international flow of ideas, goods and capital, a catch-up process was started that we can liken to the arrival of a big wave. This wave was to carry in its wake rising living standards, jobs, and wages that were especially favourable to the less skilled so rapid growth occurred with equity in the initial phase of Singapore's economic development.[5]

Yet, it is not possible to understand the huge rise in Singapore's living standards without also understanding the social forces that led to the choice of the business-friendly institutions in the first place. The factors that shape good institutions have come under scrutiny by economists and political scientists in recent years as it has come to be recognised that good institutions are fundamental in explaining the wealth of nations. Social and political influences play a vital part in explaining why pro-growth institutions were established in the first place, and identifying how these influences operate is necessary for our understanding of how the Singapore economy achieved a take-off when so many other countries have remained poor despite the ready pool of world technology. It is necessary also to understand the social and economic forces that are operative in an economy that is making a transition from catch-up growth to life in a mature economy if we are to generate future economic prosperity.

Can the economic forces that were unleashed in the first big wave, the process of catch-up growth as Singapore raced towards the world technology frontier, be counted on to generate economic prosperity for Singapore in the next 50 years? In a 4 September 2001 article titled "What's new, what's next for Singapore?" published

---

[5]The phase of growth with equity ended around the year 2000. Subsequently, the gap between the earnings of high-skill workers and low-skill workers has widened. (See the discussion of wage earnings of workers at different skill levels in Chapter 2.)

in *The Business Times*, I argued that with Singapore getting closer to the world technology frontier, growth must inevitably fall to a more moderate level that is typical among the advanced industrial economies. The same article identified three economic developments that I regarded as new for Singapore (at that point in time), each one having potentially huge socio-economic consequences. First, I argued that while the export of less-skilled-labour-intensive goods in the catch-up phase of growth raised low-skill wages and narrowed the wage gap between high-skill and low-skill workers (without the need for policy intervention such as a wage income supplement scheme for low-wage workers), economic forces would be such as to cause the wages of low-skill workers to decline in absolute and relative terms in the next stage of its economic climb. I suggested that this would come about as a result of greater competition from low-wage nations as well as from the onslaught of new technology that has a strong skill bias embedded in it. I concluded, "We have, therefore, moved from a phase of growth where economic forces tended to produce a more egalitarian society to one in which the rich tend to become richer while the poor tend to become poorer."

Second, I argued in the article that in Singapore's earlier phase of growth, actual productivity growth most likely exceeded workers' expectations. Economic growth miracles, such as the one Singapore has experienced, occur when a country that is far from the world technology frontier chooses policies that enable it to adopt the best work practices and state-of-the-art methods of production available in developed economies. I suggested in the article that "[s]uch a historically unprecedented accomplishment most likely took its participants, and economic observers, by surprise. After recording an unusually high growth rate in the catching-up phase, however, the economy must finally settle down to a more normal pace of growth in the long run." I concluded that high unemployment could result if workers do not adjust to the reality of a slower pace of growth and, accordingly, their asking wage exceeds the wage that firms can afford to pay them.

Third, I argued that while only a handful of countries adopted an outward-oriented strategy in the 1960s, many more emerging economies with varying levels of skill and capital endowments are now open to international flows of capital and goods. The integration of more emerging economies into the global trading system has occurred in tandem with a technological spurt that has brought down transport and communication costs. Consequently, this has led to a phenomenon variously termed as "international production disintegration" and "slicing of the value chain" where the many stages of production, from design to manufacturing of parts to assembly and then to marketing, can be carried out in different countries according to comparative costs. I concluded that "[t]his phenomenon, while posing a threat to Singapore's unskilled workers as the assembly of unskilled-labour-intensive parts move to low-wage countries, also presents new opportunities for Singapore." Among the new opportunities, I identified the middleman role that Singapore has traditionally played, which can take on a new form in the New Economy, and the stimulus to private entrepreneurship or enterprise brought about by more economies opening up and the IT revolution.

A decade and a half has passed since I wrote that article. The first decade of the 21st century saw Singapore confronting several major economic shocks: the end of the internet bubble, the SARS epidemic, and the global financial crisis of 2008–9.[6] The Singapore economy also sharply expanded the size of the foreign workforce in Singapore, especially in the second half of the decade, to take advantage of the opportunities for growth.[7] The increased labour force size and concomitant inflows of foreign capital delivered some years of exceptionally high growth rates in total GDP (adjusted for inflation) and low rates of both resident and total unemployment despite the slow and negative growth in total GDP in some years.

---

[6]SARS stands for Severe Acute Respiratory Syndrome, which is a viral respiratory disease.

[7]The cumulative increase in total labour force size over each half decade from 1971 onwards is as follows: 1971–75 (0.16 million workers); 1976–1980 (0.26 million workers); 1981–1985 (0.09 million workers); 1986–1990 (0.36 million workers); 1991–1995 (0.19 million workers); 1996–2000 (0.44 million workers); 2001–2005 (0.18 million workers); 2006–2010 (0.77 million workers); and 2011–2015 (0.48 million workers). Source: *Yearbook of Statistics Singapore*, Singapore Department of Statistics, various years.

The underlying forces that I identified in my 2001 article confronting Singapore are of a structural nature and might have been masked by the economic shocks and attendant policy responses to these shocks which occurred in the past decade. In this book, I seek to further develop the arguments of the 2001 article with the advantage of more than a decade worth of additional observations.

A pressing question is how to think about the sources of growth in the next decade or two? I have found that a useful way to think about Singapore's growth is to recognise that even in a well-developed economy like the U.S., not all firms operating within a narrowly defined industry are equally productive. There is a whole distribution of firm-level productivities within an industry. The most productive firms tend to be larger, sell into overseas markets, and pay similar workers more. Work by the economists Chang-Tai Hsieh and Peter Klenow has made comparisons of these firm-level productivities for China, India and the U.S. They found wider dispersion in the productivity levels in India and China as compared to the U.S. A useful 90–10 ratio of the firm at the top decile of the productivity distribution to the firm at the bottom decile in one measure is about 1.6 in India and China compared to 1.2 in the U.S.[8] Figure 0.2 illustrates a strategy to grow via narrowing the productivity dispersion of Singaporean firms within a given industry.[9] This results in a rightward shift of the productivity distribution.

Growth with equity describes reasonably well the Singapore growth experience in the first three-and-a-half decades after independence. The questions that now confront us include: Has there now been an unfavourable shift of the efficiency-equity trade-off that calls for new institutional forms to underpin a new phase of strong economic performance? What sort of growth trajectory does the population need to grasp if it is to anchor its expectations realistically and thus to avert major disappointments?

---

[8]See Table II, for the year 2005, in Chang-Tai Hsieh and Peter Klenow, 2009, "Misallocation and Manufacturing TFP in China and India," *Quarterly Journal of Economics*, 124(4): 1403–1448.

[9]On the horizontal axis, we measure a firm's productivity level taken as a ratio to the industry's average productivity level.

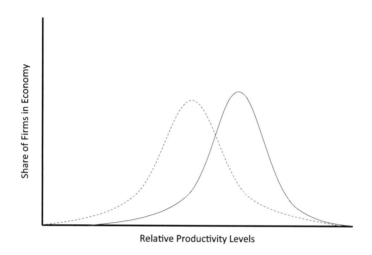

Figure 0.2:   Distribution of Productivity Levels

Note: Relative productivity level is a firm's productivity level taken as a ratio to the industry's average productivity level.

There is evidence that since the turn of the century, income gaps have widened and there is a segment of Singaporeans, the bottom quintile, whose real wage earnings — wage earnings adjusted for inflation — have not caught up and, for some, actually declined.[10] In 2007, the government introduced a wage subsidy scheme called a Workfare Income Supplement (WIS) scheme that would boost the wage earnings of low-wage workers in the bottom quintile of

---

[10] *The Key Household Income Trends, 2010* published by the Singapore Department of Statistics reports that the GINI coefficient based on original income from work per household member increased from 0.444 in the year 2000 to 0.480 in 2010. As another measure of widening income inequality, the ratio of the average income of the top quintile of resident employed households to the bottom quintile increased from 10.1 in the year 2000 to 12.9 in 2010. A report by the Housing Development Board (HDB) provides some evidence of actual declines in real wage earnings in the past decade. Chart 3.7 of the report shows the average household monthly income from work by housing type expressed in nominal terms, that is, unadjusted for inflation. For one-room HDB flat type, the value went from S$1,336 in 1998 to S$1,282. For two-room HDB flat type, the value went from S$1,691 in 1998 to S$1,718 in 2008. The total share of resident population living in one-room and two-room HDB flat types in 2008 was 3.4 percent. (Source: HDB Sample Household Survey 2008 titled *Public Housing in Singapore: Residents' Profile, Housing Satisfaction and Preferences*.)

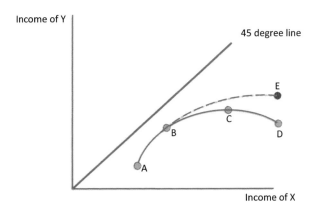

Figure 0.3: Illustration for Two Groups of Workers

the labour force.[11] Figure 0.3 illustrates for two groups of workers, called low-wage group (Y) and high-wage group (X), a phase of growth during which the incomes for both groups increased along the stretch ABC. In the segment AB, the income of low-wage workers increases relatively faster than the income of high-wage workers so that growth occurs with a declining income gap. In the segment BC, while incomes of both groups increase, the income of high-wage workers increases relatively faster so the income gap is widening. Since 2000, economic forces have worked in such a way as to cause an actual decline of real earnings for the low-wage group (Y) along the stretch CD. Wage income supplements given to low-wage workers can boost their take-home earnings while allowing high-wage workers to still enjoy an increase in their after-tax wage earnings. This would allow the economy to move along the stretch BE so that growth lifts up the incomes of both groups, mitigating the forces causing a widening income gap, with the wage income supplement scheme

---

[11]From 2010, workers aged 35 years and above with earnings no more that S$1,700 qualified for an income supplement on the condition that they worked for at least three months in any six-month period. The amount of WIS payment varied according to age and salary paid by the firm but the maximum amount of annual WIS payment in 2010 was S$2,800. The median gross monthly income from work in 2010 was S$2,710. (Source: Table 20 in *Report on Labour Force in Singapore, 2010* published by the Singapore Ministry of Manpower.)

financed by taxes on the high-wage group (X). Why growth occurred since 2000 with greater income inequality (accompanied by actual real wage declines for a segment of the labour force) and whether that is likely to continue in the future need to be understood for two reasons. First, we need to have a deep philosophical foundation for Singapore to implement policy measures to boost the earnings and employability of low-wage earners through its tax-subsidy system. Second, we need to determine the best policy instruments to achieve the objective.

What This Book is About

This book is about the importance of establishing *economic dynamism*, *economic openness*, and *economic inclusion* in the next phase of Singapore's economic development. What do we mean by economic dynamism? It is a society's ability to marshal together different stakeholders — the citizen workforce and businesses — who possibly have divergent interests, to take advantage of economic opportunities while maintaining social cohesion and a stable political equilibrium. By economic openness, we mean the integration into the global economy through the international flow of ideas, goods and services, capital, and labour. Economic inclusion involves raising the pay rate of disadvantaged workers, say relative to the median wage, so that they remain deeply engaged in regular work in the formal economy.

Singapore achieved economic dynamism in the 1960s by setting up institutions that encouraged the inflow of foreign direct investments. The improvement in the industrial relations climate lowered the calculation of risks made by multinational corporations in deciding whether to base industrial production in Singapore. Prior to the arrival of the multinational corporations, the size of the manufacturing sector was limited due to financial constraints.[12]

---

[12]The limits placed on economic development by financial constraints, particularly in the growth of the manufacturing sector, have been emphasised by the economist Francisco Buera. See Francisco J. Buera, Joseph P. Kabuski and Yonseok Shin, 2011, "Finance and Development: A Tale of Two Sectors," *American Economic Review*, 101(5): 1964–2002.

Local firms did not have the financial depth and access to funds to achieve the minimum scale of investment. The multinational corporations brought the needed capital as well as new markets and technology to produce for export. Once foreign firms entered, they could take advantage of the relative abundance of less-skilled workers to produce relatively less-skilled-labour-intensive goods such as textiles, garments, and simple electronics for the export market. Trade boosted the real wage earnings of less-skilled workers both in absolute terms as well as relative to the wage earnings of higher-skilled workers. Market forces, therefore, worked to narrow the wage gap and thus to foster social cohesion and gain political support for integrating into the global economy. The steady inflow of foreign direct investments enabled the country to overcome credit constraints faced by domestic firms even as standard technology was imported from abroad.

Economic dynamism takes a different form when the phase of catch-up growth is over. A fundamental transition is occurring in the Singapore economy. When a big gulf existed between Singapore's actual technology level and the frontier technology in the 1960s, the advantages of relative backwardness implied that the pace of technology diffusion would be fast initially. As Singapore's technology level rose, it stimulated capital investment, which provided a further stimulus to the growth of GDP per capita. As Singapore gets closer to the technology frontier, the pace of technological diffusion slows down, thus moderating Singapore's per capita GDP growth. Domestic per capita GDP growth, however, is determined by the sum of growth based on importing technologies developed abroad and growth based on indigenous innovation.[13] It is the development of indigenous innovation that can provide additional growth to the Singapore economy in its mature phase. As the stimulation of innovative activities occurs with an encouragement of startups, the economy can deliver higher growth as these startups and existing

---

[13] The importance of indigenous innovation for productivity growth in the frontier economies has been emphasised by the economist Edmund Phelps. See Edmund S. Phelps, 2013, *Mass Flourishing: How Grassroots Innovation Created Jobs, Challenge, and Change*, Princeton: Princeton University Press.

firms improve management practices, develop new products, and break into external markets.[14]

Economic integration in the global flow of ideas, goods and services, capital, and labour remains necessary as it expands GDP and provides the fiscal resources to strengthen economic inclusion. Integrating into the global economy boosts GDP through several channels. As the industry expands through selling into the external market, each firm, even though small, experiences a productivity boost that allows it to expand output. For example, industry-level trade missions into the regional economies gather useful information that each firm can take advantage of to expand sales. More productive firms also self-select into selling in export markets as they are better able to afford to cover the fixed cost of establishing export platforms. Export-oriented firms are, therefore, larger. Larger firms tend to devote more resources to screen workers and improve the quality of their workforce. As a result, larger firms pay observationally equivalent workers more. Empirical evidence suggests that neighbouring countries, after adjusting for country sizes, tend to trade more with each other.[15] The regional market provides an opportunity for domestic firms to gain the experience of selling abroad and learn from exporting. The experience gained can later help these firms to achieve international competitiveness to sell beyond regional markets. With a strong legal framework to support conflict resolutions, the Singapore economy has comparative advantage in producing nonstandard goods and services that are sensitive to opportunistic behaviour since it is difficult to write complete contracts. Product development is more likely to occur within such a strong legal and governance framework.

Demographic trends create headwinds even as Singapore moves to develop indigenous innovation. As wages increased from the 1960s,

---

[14]Research shows that variation in management practices contribute to persistent productivity differences across firms and countries. See Nicholas Bloom and John Van Reenen, 2010, "Why Do Management Practices Differ across Firms and Countries?" *Journal of Economic Perspectives*, 24(1): 203–224.

[15]See Robert C. Feenstra, 2016, *Advanced International Trade: Theory and Evidence*, second edition, Princeton: Princeton University Press.

the opportunity cost of having another child also increased. While higher incomes mean that people can afford to have more children, it has been observed that the total fertility rate tends to decline as countries become richer suggesting that the substitution effect dominates the income effect of higher wages.[16] People invest more in raising the human capital of their children even as family size shrinks. A shrinking workforce, while it increases the capital intensity in the short run, ultimately leads to lower investment as capital needs decline. What poses a challenge for Singapore is that an economy with an older age structure appears to generate slower productivity growth.[17] One reason is that the lower labour force participation rate among older workers limits the extent of knowledge transfer from older and more experienced workers to younger workers. Another reason is that the pace of innovation tends to slow down due to a decline in the supply of entrepreneurs. To generate economic prosperity in the mature phase, Singapore will have to adopt a two-pronged approach to boost total fertility and manage a controlled inflow of immigrants to keep the population from shrinking.

The Singapore economy has transited from a phase of growth when the efficiency-equity frontier moved favourably to another phase of growth when a given level of equity corresponds to slower economic growth. What is needed now is to develop a system of social insurance that is fiscally sustainable. A political equilibrium must be achieved that would allow an increase in the supply of entrepreneurs to develop indigenous innovation in the face of the declining citizen population. Productivity growth driven by indigenous innovation is needed to provide the fiscal resources to lift up the pay rate of the economically disadvantaged. An innovative economy also facilitates social mobility if the state invests in raising the cognitive and non-cognitive abilities of children from disadvantaged families and expose them to role models of successful innovators. By providing them a

---

[16]See Gary S. Becker, 1991, *A Treatise on the Family*, enlarged edition, Cambridge, MA: Harvard University Press.
[17]See Nicole Maestas, Kathleen J. Mullen, and David Powell, 2016, "The Effect of Population Aging on Economic Growth, the Labor Force and Productivity," NBER Working Paper No. 22452.

good chance of becoming successful innovators despite coming from low-income families, the index of social mobility can improve given the uncertainty inherent in new business ventures.[18] Basic to gaining political support to embrace economic openness is the recognition that a social surplus is created when people with different abilities and skill levels specialise in activities in which they have comparative advantage.

The nature of what the good life is for an individual depends upon the type of society that the person lives in. In the first phase of growth, it was possible for workers across the whole skills distribution to hold jobs that delivered rising wages propelled by market forces until around 2000. Since then, policy intervention in the form of the Workfare Income Supplement scheme has been necessary to foster economic inclusion. The next phase of growth requires indigenous innovation that is likely to come along with greater creative destruction and more frequent disruptions to jobs and wages. It is, nevertheless, still possible to envision careers that are fulfilling if the economy generates for each individual the potential to achieve his or her dreams. Such an economy is apt to be one that is dynamic and inclusive even though individuals can expect to face more transitions in their career over a lifetime.

---

[18] Alex Bell, Raj Chetty, Xavier Jaravel, Neviana Petkova, and John Van Reneen, 2017, "Who Becomes an Inventor in America? The Importance of Exposure to Innovation," NBER Working Paper No. 24062.

Part I

The Aggregate Economy and Its Heterogeneity

Chapter 1

Four Things that Matter

Just as good readings of a person's blood pressure and cholesterol levels give indications of a generally healthy body over a period of time, we can identify economic indicators that might give us an idea of how healthy an economy is. Four economic indicators are identified: the real GDP per capita gives us a measure of a country's standard of living; the unemployment rate gives a measure of how well the job market is functioning in providing jobs to its citizens; the rate of inflation gives a measure of how fast the cost of living is rising; and the wage gap gives a measure of how wide is the extent of inequality among workers. In this chapter, we examine why these four indicators matter for the general health of an economy.

Living Standards

Economists use an indicator called the real Gross Domestic Product (GDP) as a measure of the total amount of goods and services produced within an economy during a period of time, say, a year. When this amount is divided by the size of the population, we obtain the real GDP per capita, the average amount of goods and services produced per person, in a given year. If this quantity is found to be rising steadily over a sufficiently long period of time, like a few decades, it is probably indicative that life is steadily getting better for the median citizen — the citizen right in the middle of the income distribution. The qualifier "probably" is used because economic growth could, in theory, be very unequal, in which case the gains could go disproportionately to a small fraction of the population even though living standards for the median citizen are stagnant or even declining. Nevertheless, in the Singapore experience, the fruits of economic growth have been broadly shared so life for every citizen has generally become better over the first three-and-a-half decades since it became independent. However, there are signs of stagnation or even decline in wage earnings for the bottom quintile of the population since 2000.[1]

Figure 1.1 plots Singapore's real GDP per capita since 1960, expressed in constant Singapore dollars. It is a story of rapid economic growth. Why is economic growth desirable? The monthly income of a typical citizen in Singapore was about S$340 (measured in 2000 market prices) in 1960.[2] This would just be a third of what

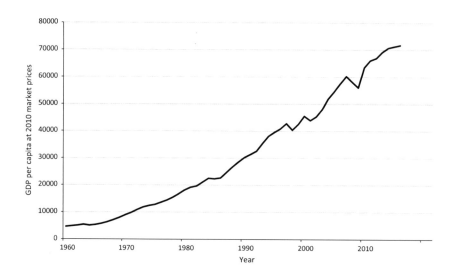

Figure 1.1:   Singapore's Standard of Living, 1960–2016

Source: Department of Statistics, Singapore.

---

[1]The bulk of income for the bottom quintile of the income distribution derives from wage earnings rather than from unearned income such as dividends and capital gains from holding stocks.

[2]This is obtained by taking S$4,085, which is the 1960's real GDP per capita measured in year 2000 market prices, and dividing by 12.

we regard today as what a person at the bottom decile of our income distribution (the poorest 10 percent of the population) should at least earn to get by on a fairly austere lifestyle. So Singaporeans were generally poor in 1960 even though most lived above the poverty line used by the World Bank to define extreme poverty, namely, US\$1 per day per person (measured at the 1985 purchasing power parity exchange rate). Being poor meant that certain basic amenities we take for granted nowadays were out of reach of most people — televisions, telephones, air-conditioning, etc. Eating out in a restaurant would be a rare treat. It would be uncommon for a parent to enlist a child in an enrichment programme such as a ballet class. Access to credit from commercial banks, whether in the form of a loan to acquire a consumer durable or to launch a business idea, was limited, so informal credit arrangements developed among kinsfolk and neighbours.

Enjoying a higher standard of living, on the other hand, means that the opportunity set facing each individual is enlarged so that he/she can buy more goods and services than before. Moreover, it is not just that a richer person can buy larger quantities of the same goods. One important component of growth is that more varieties of goods and services are introduced into the economy. The typical household in Singapore today can buy certain types of goods and services that were simply not available in 1960 such as a DVD player. With higher earnings that come with a higher standard of living, workers are able to put more aside for savings that they can later use for unexpected events such as a family member falling seriously ill. A very important concomitant of a steady rise in living standards is that people are better equipped to handle adverse changes in circumstances affecting them or their family members as their increased resources provide them better insurance. They are better equipped to cope with risk as they become richer. Having more resources also means that individuals are better able to finance their own human capital accumulation and those of their children. Parents can afford to send their children to enrichment classes and sponsor overseas trips to widen their children's international exposure.

Being rich also has important community effects. When most citizens of a country enjoy a high standard of living, more resources can be drawn upon through the tax system to finance a high standard of public goods such as public libraries and national parks that people can enjoy. The public health system is improved as more resources can be channelled to provide a higher quality of basic healthcare for all. Both public and private hospitals also invest in better medical equipment and technology and pharmaceutical companies supply better drugs for ailments as people are able to afford a higher quality of healthcare. The quality of public transport improves as the government has more resources to build better roads and other physical infrastructure. The quality of public education also improves as more fiscal resources are available to pay more qualified teachers, raise the teacher-student ratio, and invest in information technology and laboratory facilities.

What we have said so far concerns what it means to be rich. However, Singaporeans started off being relatively poor in 1960. In relation to the U.S., Singapore started off at self-government being at 15 percent of the U.S. standard of living. Today, we have reached about 140 percent of the U.S. level.[3] To get from being relatively poor to the present standard of living means that we have had to grow very fast. One pertinent question is whether there is anything good about experiencing growth itself. If you have a choice between being a citizen of a country that starts off at a fairly high standard of living but grows rather slowly every year, and being a citizen of a country that starts off being relatively poor but grows at a very rapid rate so that over your lifetime the present value of your income is the same, which would you choose? According to neoclassical theory, one should be indifferent about the two options given one's preferences.

---

[3]According to the Penn World Table version 9.0, Singapore's per capita (expenditure-side) real GDP in 2011 US$ on a (chained) purchasing power parity (PPP) adjusted basis is US$2,664 in 1960 and US$72,670 in 2014 compared to the United States' US$17,600 in 1960 and US$52,292 in 2014, respectively. See Robert C. Feenstra, Robert Inklaar and Marcel P. Timmer, 2015, "The Next Generation of the Penn World Table," *American Economic Review*, 105(10): 3150–3182, available for download at www.ggdc.net/pwt

With perfect capital markets, a citizen in the country that starts off relatively poor can always borrow to attain the desired consumption profile, consuming more than income in the early stage of growth and repaying debt in the later stage of growth. The economist Benjamin Friedman, however, has found from a careful historical study of both advanced and developing countries that, in fact, people seem to be more magnanimous to each other, are more tolerant of diversity, and have a greater commitment to social justice and democratic institutions, so the societies they live in function better on the whole, when their growth rates are high.[4] On the other hand, when growth slows down and, worse, when the economy is stagnant, there appears to be a retreat along these moral dimensions of the society's character.

In the Singapore experience, it would appear that the phenomenal growth rates we experienced, particularly in the first two decades of growth after gaining independence in 1965, far exceeded what its citizens would have dared to hope. There were not many historical precedents when Singapore, along with the East Asian economies of Hong Kong, South Korea, and Taiwan, began their economic take-off in the post-war period apart from Japan. Moreover, the set of institutions that the country established and its commitment to open itself up to the free international flow of goods and capital were not conventional at the time in development thinking, which emphasised import substitution and infant industry protection. The laws and institutions that gave foreign enterprises the confidence to build factories and employ workers in Singapore to produce for the world market set the country off on a high growth trajectory as it raced towards the world technology frontier. Singaporeans found their lives improving year after year and there must have been a strong sense of optimism among workers and their families. This, no doubt, acted to strengthen a sense of social cohesion in a multi-racial society. However, this sense of optimism that was tied up, not with higher income levels per se, but with rapid growth itself — the feeling

---

[4]See Benjamin M. Friedman, 2005, *The Moral Consequences of Economic Growth*, New York: Alfred A. Knopf.

that one was on a steep escalator that was moving up fast — could well turn into pessimism when the growth itself slows down despite having attained a higher level of income. One can be rich and yet be very unhappy because life is not improving, at any rate, as fast as before.

A crucial question that confronts Singapore at this later phase of its development, as it makes a transition to being a mature economy, is whether the growth rates of the five decades after independence can be repeated. Does economic theory provide a useful guide for us to think about what the future growth path of Singapore might be like? Finding the correct answer to this question can make a big difference to the moral character of the economy that will go beyond enjoying a higher standard of living today than 50 years ago. What growth rates are realistic and what economic model would deliver such growth paths? Historical experience of today's advanced industrial economies since the Industrial Revolution suggests that there is a process called conditional convergence.[5] This refers to the fact that, controlling for factors such as a nation's savings rate, the average number of years of schooling, and the share of trade in GDP, countries grow at roughly the same rate over the long run. Countries that save more, have a better educated workforce, and are more open to trade, tend to be richer but do not exhibit permanently higher growth rates. This suggests that Singapore is unlikely to deliver similar growth rates as in previous decades. If we take two percent growth of GDP per capita that the U.S. experienced in the last century as a long-run benchmark, Singapore's challenge is to add to productivity growth derived from imported technology another source of growth derived from indigenous innovation. Introducing new brands of products, developing higher-quality products, and improving methods of production to lower costs by new startups will form part of the new engine of growth. Carrying out such innovative activities requires a steady flow of entrepreneurs. Having a better-educated workforce increases the supply of individuals who

---

[5]Robert J. Barro and Xavier Sala-i-Martin, 2004, *Economic Growth*, second edition, Cambridge, MA: MIT Press.

are capable of navigating new and novel situations brought about by new general purpose technologies like digitisation. On the other hand, a shrinking workforce due to below replacement total fertility rates reduces the supply of potential entrepreneurs since new ideas come from people. Singapore will have to be a place that attracts creators of new startups to work in Singapore to offset this decrease in supply. The resulting larger GDP expands the tax base to provide the needed tax revenue to support wage subsidy and training programmes for citizens.

Jobs

There are important non-pecuniary rewards from work. Research shows that people who lose their jobs lose something more than the wage earnings they forgo. The personal habits that come from a work routine provide a rhythm to living and a sense of fulfilment that one is doing something worthwhile. Character traits like being punctual, having the perseverance to keep at solving problems, having the imagination to create new ideas, and having the ability to manage inter-personal conflicts are all developed at the workplace.

When a country is relatively poor, as Singapore was at independence in 1965, there are fewer job opportunities.[6] At any rate, there are fewer career jobs available. People have an inherent desire to attain higher levels of responsibility in their job, which is why career jobs provide promotion ladders. Dedication to one's tasks and accomplishing the goals equated to a given level of responsibility provide a sense of challenge. When supervisors deem a worker to have done well and recommend a promotion, the feeling of being rewarded is palpable. However, to have a reliable supply of good career jobs requires an economy to have a steady pace of firm creation that outstrips firm closures. This means that in the process of economic

---

[6] According to the Penn World Table version 9.0, in the year 1965, Singapore's per capita (expenditure-side) real GDP in 2011 US\$ on a (chained) purchasing power parity (PPP) adjusted basis is US\$3,263 compared to US\$21,021 for the U.S. See Feenstra, et al., *op. cit.*

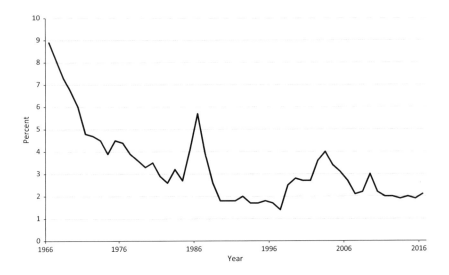

Figure 1.2:   Singapore's Annual Average Unemployment Rate, 1966–2016
Source: Singapore Ministry of Manpower.

restructuring, an environment must be created to facilitate the entry of new firms even as old firms exit.

Figure 1.2 shows the evolution of Singapore's unemployment rate from 1966 to 2016. The unemployment rate declines when the number of workers having access to a job exceeds the number of employed workers who either get retrenched or quit to look for another job. Singapore's decision to woo multinational firms as a key platform of its economic strategy, after the prospect of a Malaysian Common Market failed to materialise with independence in 1965, provided the economic environment for rapid firm entry. In the late 1960s and 1970s, many of the new firms were relatively less-skilled-labour-intensive firms in such industries as textiles and garments and simple assembly-line electronics. The multinational firms brought along with them technologies and work processes that were implemented on the factory floors. Without requiring a high level of education, many of the jobs created in Singapore could be filled simply by less-skilled workers with a keen attitude to learn and who would not sabotage the machinery put in place on the factory floor.

Wages earned by many of the Singaporean workers in the 1960s and 1970s would not be high compared to their counterparts in the Western economies. In the decade after independence, it was the low cost of labour coupled with a hardworking workforce that attracted the multinational firms to locate plants in Singapore. Nevertheless, the abundant job opportunities created provided Singaporeans with a source of steady income and the means to plan for a stable family life. There was the opportunity to form the habits necessary to hold on to a steady job even if the pay was not high. Moreover, learning on the job raised the human capital of Singaporean workers who missed out on the opportunity to go for formal higher education. Promotions allowed workers to rise up from being production floor workers to supervisory positions.

The huge investment the government made in providing vocational training also helped to raise the skill level of workers. The enlarged stock of human capital, acquired both on the job as well as through the vocational training provided by government and industry, served to make Singapore increasingly more attractive to firms producing more skill-intensive and physical capital-intensive products. (Physical capital tended to complement skills.) A process of creative destruction occurred with firms higher up the value chain replacing lower value-added firms that exited. Along with industrial restructuring, new jobs were created that paid higher wages so median wage earnings were gradually raised as years passed.

The multinational firms that were based in Singapore tended to encourage the growth of local small and medium-sized enterprises which supplied the industrial inputs required by foreign affiliates based in Singapore. This means both the emergence of a class of local entrepreneurs as well as new employment opportunities for Singaporean workers. Local firms varied in their productivity levels. The growth of a network of supply chains allowed some local firms to acquire the financial depth and technical expertise to produce not only to serve foreign affiliates based in Singapore, but also to export their products. A large number, however, remained insufficiently productive to have the means to cover the fixed cost of setting up the infrastructure needed to break into overseas markets and therefore served only the domestic market.

Workers' personal job satisfaction and the dedication to their job raised labour productivity, which boosted labour demand. However, the determination of overall employment and wage levels depend not only on individual productivity but also on the industrial relations climate. In the early 1960s, labour strikes were a common feature leading to the loss of many productive man-hours. Legislation taking the form of the Employment Act of 1968 and Industrial Relations (Amendment) Act, also of 1968, were key initiatives that helped to promote industrial peace. The number of labour strikes dropped dramatically by the late 1960s. The Economic Development Board, initially set up in 1960, reorganised itself to pursue a policy of attracting multinational firms to set up plants in Singapore. The emphasis on job creation, particularly in the face of withdrawal of British troops based in Singapore which was expected to lead to a non-negligible decline in GDP, helped to provide tangible benefits to workers as the labour market tightened. This enabled the labour unions to win over the support of their members to welcome the inflows of foreign direct investments to produce for export. In the 1960s, this was an unconventional policy as import substitution was still the favoured policy of countries that had recently won independence from their colonial masters.

Becoming integrated into the global economy brought the benefits of access to technology and market. However, becoming economically open to the world market also subjected the economy to adverse shocks emanating from overseas from time to time. The oil price shocks of 1973 and 1979 brought inflationary pressures along with an unfavourable trade-off between real wages and employment, a situation termed stagflation by the economist Paul Samuelson. The willingness of workers to accept real wage cuts to save jobs enabled the Singapore economy to ride through the two oil crises without massive loss of jobs. The National Wages Council, set up in 1972, provided the institution for employers, representatives of labour unions, and the government (itself a major public sector employer) to take into account pertinent macroeconomic factors in the negotiation of wages. The so-called tripartism that grew out of a national-level effort at generating welfare gains for rank-and-file workers while preserving a generally business-friendly environment strengthened trust among the tripartite partners.

The high level of trust among the tripartite partners became a huge asset when the Singapore economy was buffeted by a severe recession in 1985. A major plank in the fight to save jobs took the form of a major cut in employers' cost of hiring through the reduction of employers' contribution to workers' retirement funds called the Central Provident Fund (CPF). The 15-percentage point CPF rate cut, amounting to a decline of about 12 percent of wage costs, was accepted by workers on the understanding that when the economy recovered wage levels would be restored. Indeed, the economy did recover and CPF contribution rates were gradually restored although to what was regarded as a more sustainable rate of 20 percent, down from the initial rate of 25 percent prior to the CPF rate cut. It can be argued that the wage cuts helped close the output gap and returned the economy to a trend growth path during the catch-up phase.[7]

Now, as Singapore transits to becoming a mature economy without the tailwinds of catch-up growth, what room is left for counter-recessionary measures to save jobs when adverse economic shocks hit the economy? I argue in this book that entrepreneurial startups as well as small and medium-sized enterprises need to break into overseas markets in order to enjoy economies of scale. This is so even in the face of threats of trade wars. With this reliance on external markets to support indigenous innovation, there will inevitably be recessionary shocks that hit the economy from time to time. When Singapore was hit by a decline in external demand during the 2008–09 global financial crisis, the cost-cutting measures to minimise firms' retrenchment of workers included a Jobs Credit scheme funded by drawing upon reserves. After the economy rebounded in 2010, the

---

[7]At given goods prices, a cut in the nominal wage levels made it more profitable for firms to increase employment and thus expand actual output supply. The output gap is the shortfall of the actual output supply relative to the economy's potential output.

government returned the reserves. To prepare for future external shocks, fiscal policy should aim to generate budgetary surpluses during exceptionally good times so that it has the fiscal resources to draw upon to support cost-cutting measures and finance wage subsidies during downturns. The arrival of robotics and artificial intelligence has both disruptive and wage-boosting effects. Robots that add to the human workforce and substitute for them tend to depress wages and lead to employment decline. However, advances in artificial intelligence also enable workers to increase their work productivity and thus boost their pay. We are likely to see both types of robots being employed in future so government efforts to help match workers who lose their jobs to firms that will have the incentive to hire them will take on greater importance.[8] Employment protection legislation that makes it costly to lay off workers tends to make firms cautious about creating job vacancies in the first place. As a result, while stronger employment protection legislation leads to reduced job destruction rates, it also leads to a slower pace of job creation. The result is that, while the unemployment rate is not necessarily higher because of stronger employment protection, the fraction of the long-term unemployed tends to be higher. Long-term unemployment leads to a serious loss of skills and habits necessary for productive work. It is preferable to have a social insurance system that strongly encourages the creation of new jobs and reduces the typical duration of unemployment.

Inflation

The inflation rate measures the rate of change in a country's general price level. Singapore's central bank, the Monetary Authority of Singapore (MAS), does not have an explicit inflation target such as that of New Zealand's central bank, which is required to achieve inflation rates, measured as annual increases in the consumer price index (CPI), of between 1 to 3 percent on average in the medium

---

[8]The Adapt and Grow programmes involve efforts to build a pool of firms that are ready to hire retrenched and unemployed workers through providing the firms employment and training subsidies.

term.[9] The MAS includes in its mission statement an aim to "promote sustained non-inflationary economic growth".[10]

While the MAS does not have an explicit inflation target, its conduct of monetary policy to support non-inflationary economic growth does not, in practice, aim at zero average inflation rate. There is a good reason why central banks around the world typically do not aim at a zero rate of inflation. To see why, suppose that there are two sectors in the economy, a traded-good sector and a non-traded good sector. The general price level, let's say the CPI, is the weighted average of the traded-good price index and the non-traded good price index where the weights are given by the share of a typical consumption basket going to the two goods. Imagine that, for some exogenous reason, there is a decline in the demand for the non-traded good leading to a fall in dollar price of the non-traded good. There would be a retrenchment of workers employed in the non-traded good sector. In order for the retrenched workers to be absorbed into employment in the traded-good sector, and thus avoid an increase in unemployment, the real product wage in terms of the traded good would have to decline. However, because nominal wages, that is, dollar wages, tend to be rigid downwards, the real wage cut would typically have to be effected by higher inflation. In this way, inflation helps to grease the wheel and save jobs. In other words, real wage cuts to save jobs are achieved by positive inflation at given nominal wage levels.

It is sometimes thought that the central bank can engineer an economic boom by creating surprise inflation. The thinking here is that, given the lag in gathering information about the general price level, a producer who observes an increase in the dollar price of the good that he is selling is led to attribute at least a portion of the

---

[9]A public contract is negotiated between the New Zealand government and the Reserve Bank of New Zealand called the Policy Targets Agreement (PTA). The inflation target of 1 to 3 percent given in the text is specified in the PTA signed in December 2008.

[10]The full mission statement of the MAS is the following: "Our mission is to promote sustained non-inflationary economic growth, and a sound and progressive financial centre."

increase to an improvement in his relative price leading him to move
up his supply curve. As all producers act likewise, the overall level
of economic activity is elevated above the normal level. Evidence in
support of this theory of producers being confused about general as
opposed to relative price increases is mixed at best, and it does not
appear that Singapore's central bank relies on this mechanism to
stimulate economic activity.

In economies where the private sector is over-leveraged and over-
burdened by high levels of debt, such as some of the Western
economies in the current economic climate find themselves, surprise
inflation can reduce the real value of private-sector debt and boost
effective demand. Such a policy to fight recessions, however, amounts
to redistributing wealth from creditors to debtors. In Singapore,
retirement wealth via the CPF is not indexed against inflation
so a burst of unanticipated inflation will reduce the real value of
accumulated savings in the CPF.

Generally speaking, Singapore's central bank has aimed to achieve
a predictable and stable rate of inflation even if it has not spelt out an
explicit inflation target. It conducts monetary policy by influencing
the exchange rate index based on a basket of currencies of its major
trading partners within an undisclosed band. A stronger domestic
currency leads to lower inflation via a direct channel by making
foreign goods consumed by Singaporeans cheaper, and via an indirect
channel by weakening effective demand from overseas buyers. There
is less use of discretionary monetary policy as a means to fight
recessions. Instead, the lowering of wage costs, via reductions in
the employers' CPF contribution rates to fight the 1985 recession
and direct wage subsidies given to firms in the Jobs Credit scheme
implemented in 2009, has appeared to be the preferred policy option.

What are the costs and benefits of anticipated inflation? One
cost, termed a shoe-leather cost, refers to the fact that a higher
inflation rate leads households and businesses to hold less cash at
each moment. To meet transaction needs, they therefore have to visit
ATMs and banks more frequently to withdraw cash thus incurring
resource costs. In extreme cases, such as during hyperinflations, shoe-
leather costs can be quite substantial. At the inflation rates that

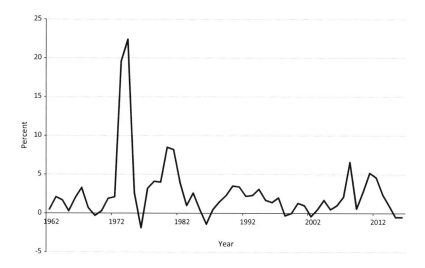

Figure 1.3: Singapore's Annual Average Inflation Rate, 1962–2016
Source: Department of Statistics, Singapore.
Note: Inflation rate is calculated using Consumer Price Index.

Singapore has experienced (see Figure 1.3), this cost does not seem to be prohibitive.

High expected inflation can work through the tax system, which is generally non-indexed to inflation, to incur substantially higher costs. An obvious channel is sometimes called tax bracket creep, which is when higher inflation bumps up an individual's tax liability into a higher marginal tax rate bracket. This would act to create labour supply distortions. In places where nominal interest earnings are taxed, a higher rate of inflation leads to a lower after-tax real rate of interest. Since it is the latter that is the relevant rate of return individuals use to decide on how much to save, a higher inflation rate can also lead to lower private savings. Under current tax laws in Singapore, interest earnings from savings placed in local and qualifying full banks are tax-exempt so this channel is not relevant.

Governments can collect tax revenue via an inflation tax, called seigniorage. In effect, new dollar notes that cost little for the government to print can be used to pay public sector workers and finance government purchases. In countries where tax evasion is high, the printing press provides the government a means to collect tax revenue using the inflation tax. At inflation rates common in the developed economies in the past two to three decades, it is safe to say that governments have not resorted to seigniorage as a means to boost tax revenues. Certainly, the Singapore government has not resorted to this means of collecting tax revenues.

Central banks, through the use of instruments like the setting of short-term interest rate, seek to control the inflation rate. In Singapore, as mentioned before, the preferred instrument used is management of the exchange rate index against the currencies of major trading partners. Under normal circumstances, these instruments are sufficient to achieve the goal of price stability. However, there have been historical episodes in monetary history when central banks have had to resort to substantial increases in the monetary base to fulfil their role as lender of last resort to the system of commercial banks. An example is the recent financial crisis of 2008 when the collapse of Lehman Brothers led the U.S. Federal Reserve System, America's central bank, to substantially increase the monetary base as heightened uncertainty led financial firms and banks to hold excess reserves. This policy of making a substantial injection of liquidity into the banking system when credit tightened is partly the result of a lesson drawn by the economists Milton Friedman and Anna Schwartz from studying the causes of the Great Depression in the U.S. in the 1930s. In their monumental work published in 1963 entitled *A Monetary History of the United States, 1867–1960*, they argued that it was the failure of the Federal Reserve Bank to expand the monetary base in the face of a sharp drop in the money multiplier that caused a recession to turn into a depression.[11] In 2009, when Singapore felt the impact of the financial crisis emanating from the U.S., the MAS injected a higher level of Singapore dollar liquidity into the banking system.[12]

---

[11]The reference is to Milton Friedman and Anna Schwartz, 1963, *A Monetary History of the United States, 1867–1960*, Princeton: Princeton University Press.

[12]In addition, the MAS entered into a US$30 billion swap arrangement with the U.S. Federal Reserve to provide U.S. dollar liquidity. (Source: Monetary Authority of Singapore, *Financial Stability Review*, November 2009, page 37.)

For over two decades after the Volcker disinflationary policy brought in an era of low and stable inflation rates in the U.S., central banks around the world also came to focus on their primary aim of maintaining price stability and using the short-term interest rate as a policy instrument. As the mature economies of the developed world have found themselves faced with near zero short-term interest rates after the global financial crisis in 2008-09, it has become less clear what set of tools is available to fight recessions. With free international capital mobility, the near zero short-term interest rate in the advanced industrial economies places a limitation on Singapore's conduct of counter-recessionary policy.[13]

Another future challenge is the following. Even under conditions of fairly low and stable inflation, the economist William Baumol has called attention to the fact that prices of labour-intensive services in health care and education have increased while manufactured good prices such as computers have declined.[14] This appears to be a general phenomenon in the advanced economies. The mechanism leading to more costly services compared to manufactured goods has got to do with the relatively slower productivity gains in services compared to manufacturing. As continuous improvements in the production of computers occur, for example, manufacturing wages are pulled up. Since the demand for many services remains high, the need to raise wages to retain and attract workers in the less productive services sector result in their charging higher prices. It is likely that Singaporeans will face relatively more expensive healthcare and education services in future. In its regulatory and

---

[13]Suppose that inflation expectations are well anchored in a normal environment with positive nominal short-term interest rates domestically and overseas. In the face of a negative external shock that reduces Singapore's aggregate demand, there will be a downward pressure on domestic interest rates which will prompt capital outflows and a weakening of the Singapore dollar. The currency depreciation increases Singapore's international competitiveness and brings about an economic recovery through boosting net exports. This channel is, however, constrained when the domestic and overseas short-term interest rates are both already close to zero.

[14]See William J. Baumol, 2012, *The Cost Disease: Why Computers Get Cheaper and Health Care Doesn't*, New Haven: Yale University Press.

supervisory role, the Monetary Authority of Singapore also plays an important part in helping to develop the venture capital industry to support the financing of startups in Singapore's next phase of growth. The development of the financial sector to channel savings to finance new business ventures is critical to supporting indigenous innovation.

Wage Inequality

When an individual makes a decision whether to devote an additional year to schooling, he takes account of the likelihood that the job that he is able to do with the additional human capital will pay him better. Wage inequality, here measured as the wage differential between a low-skill and a high-skill worker, therefore, serves as an incentive for the individual to acquire higher skills. Having an economic system that equalises pay for everyone regardless of productivity will therefore sap away any drive to acquire higher skills.

Suppose that the market rewards workers according to their labour productivities. There is a pool of workers whose labour productivities can be arranged in a continuum. We then have an endogenously determined wage income distribution with the most productive workers higher up the skills continuum being paid multiple times more than a less-skilled worker much lower down the skills continuum. Does this matter? Is there any basis for society to agree on a set of rules built into its institutions, more specifically through its tax-subsidy system, to reduce the net take-home pay of those higher up in the skills distribution to finance wage subsidies to low-wage workers?

A helpful way to frame this discussion goes back to a formulation by the political philosopher John Rawls who conceived of a society as being made up of different individuals engaged in collaborative production and exchange thus generating significant social surplus or social dividends.[15] In the absence of a tax-subsidy system, such

---

[15]See John Rawls, 1971, *A Theory of Justice*, Cambridge, MA: Harvard University Press. The economist Edmund Phelps has emphasised the central importance of the social surplus from collaboration among different members of society in

a society would distribute that social surplus based upon labour productivities and preferences for the different goods produced by people with different levels of skills. Yet we may owe something to each other that would make the more skilled individuals reason that they would be willing, through the tax-subsidy system, to pay taxes to boost the earnings of those at the lower end of the skills continuum.[16]

One might reason that if we could hypothetically go back to the moment before a society is formed and write a social contract, not knowing the position one would take in that society, we might end up agreeing on a tax-subsidy system that would make the worst-off as well off as he could be. In this conceptualisation, it is important to note that at the moment of writing the contract, the nature of the skills continuum itself is unknowable so that it is not possible to assign a probability distribution to the allocation of skills to individuals. There is a lower bound that one might attach to how far the tax-subsidy system would reduce the net take-home pay of the more skilled. This lower bound is determined by noting that, in principle, an individual could withdraw from that society to go it alone. The tax rate, therefore, could not go higher than the level that would leave any individual just as well off as if he operated in isolation.

The philosopher John Rawls worked out a particular post-tax-subsidy system giving a level of wage inequality based upon a Difference Principle. To see how much this level of wage inequality is that can be justified by the social contract, we can start off initially with a convenient case where taxes and subsidies are such as to leave equality among all the members of society. This would leave the more skilled in society with little incentive to work and produce so that by

---

building upon Rawls' work in his proposal for a national wage subsidy scheme in the U.S. See Edmund S. Phelps, 1997, *Rewarding Work: How to Restore Participation and Self-Support to Free Enterprise*, Cambridge, MA: Harvard University Press.

[16] "What we owe to each other" is the title of a book by the philosopher Thomas Scanlon. See Thomas M. Scanlon, 1998, *What We Owe To Each Other*, Cambridge, MA: Harvard University Press.

reducing their tax rates we would be able to expand total output. By expanding output and so the tax base, low-wage workers can actually increase their post-subsidy earnings despite their reduced share and increased wage inequality. The level of wage inequality that can be justified is the level beyond which the incentive effect of lower taxes on the more skilled cannot expand total output sufficiently to offset the reduced share of the less skilled.

When widening wage inequalities occur with stagnant or declining wage earnings of low-wage workers, signs of society's malfunctions can be accentuated. When the pay is so low that the lifestyle of the breadwinner is so distant from what is regarded as a normal middle-income lifestyle, pessimism sets in. Strains are placed on family life; it is difficult for parents to serve as good role models to their children. Parents' investments in both the cognitive and non-cognitive skills of their children, especially in their early years, play a big role in influencing their adult economic outcomes.[17] Societies that fail to arrest the problem of big widening of the wage gap early on pay the price of future adult workers with weaker work motivation and ability to acquire skills. This argument is strengthened by the fact that low pay is often associated with poor job holding. A wage subsidy to firms for every low-wage worker they hire therefore can act to boost both the low-wage workers' take-home pay as well as their employment.

Figure 1.4 shows that the index of wage inequality actually declined from 1978 to about 2000. In the following decade, this measure of wage inequality began to rise. This suggests that since independence, growth occurred with equity in the first three-and-a-half decades. However, forces such as a shift of comparative advantage away from unskilled-labour-intensive goods and the onslaught of skill-biased technological progress have acted to reverse this trend since 2000. Economic openness to the international flow of ideas, goods, capital, and labour has been a central pillar of Singapore's

---

[17]See James J. Heckman, 2012, *Giving Kids a Fair Chance*, Cambridge, MA: MIT Press.

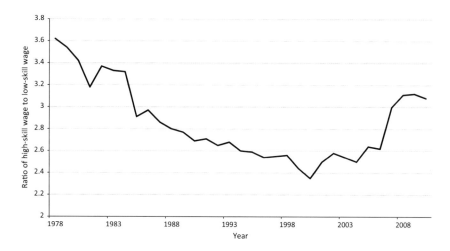

Figure 1.4:   Measure of Singapore's Wage Inequality, 1978–2010

Source: Department of Statistics, Singapore and Singapore Ministry of Manpower.

Note: The measure of wage inequality is computed from various issues of Singapore Yearbook of Statistics and Report of Wages in Singapore. It is constructed as the ratio of high-skill wage to low-skill wage.

economic development. This has propelled the catch-up growth that has lifted average living standards for nearly half a century. Social and political support for maintaining economic openness is easier to achieve when the less well-off in society actually find their own relative positions to the more skilled narrowing. That support is somewhat weakened when the less well-off in society fall behind economically, not only relatively but for some also absolutely.

A view of wage earnings driven by labour productivities and labour supplies provides a useful framework for thinking about the determination of wage income distribution. However, economists have also pointed to other models of the labour market that may help to explain other determinants of wage earnings having particularly to do with the income share of the top one to ten percent in the income distribution. In a useful survey of the income of the top earners, by the economists Anthony Atkinson, Thomas Piketty, and Emmanuel Saez, some data are collected of the Singapore economy over the long run.[18] In 1949, the top one percent of income earners in Singapore earned 10.38 percent of total income before tax and excluding realised capital gains. By 2005, this share had risen to 13.28 percent. As a comparison, the corresponding shares for 1949 and 2005, respectively, are 10.95 percent and 17.42 percent (the U.S.), 11.47 percent and 14.25 percent (the United Kingdom), 7.89 percent and 9.20 percent (Japan), 9.01 percent and 8.73 percent (France), 7.64 percent and 6.28 percent (Sweden), and 7.71 percent and 7.08 percent (Finland).

The Anglo-Saxon economies (represented by the U.S. and the United Kingdom) are most unequal by this measure while the Scandinavian economies (represented by Sweden and Finland) are least unequal with France and Japan in between. It would appear that Singapore's inequality measured by the share of the top one percent in total income is closer to the Anglo-Saxon economies. From 1965 to 1997, the top one percent income earners in Singapore earned about 10 percent of total income before tax. From 1998, that share began to rise to about 15 percent in 2002 before receding to above 13 percent in 2005.[19]

Explanations for incomes at the top appeal to three theories. A tournament theory conceives of the pay for the top job in a corporation, say that of the CEO, as being set to create strong competition among potential insiders, say the Vice-Presidents, to get that job. Another theory is that of pay for superstars, which sees a modern CEO as competing in a global market for talent. It is not only talented sportsmen and actors and singers who command extremely high pay but also talented lawyers, accountants, and CEOs who are seen to compete in a large global market. A third theory is an explicitly political theory that sees limits to the maximum pay that can be earned by top income earners in a given society being strongly influenced by the political environment. A (perhaps invisible) ceiling is set on how much is socially and politically acceptable. Another

---

[18]See Anthony B. Atkinson, Thomas Piketty, and Emmanuel Saez, 2011, "Top Incomes in the Long Run of History," *Journal of Economic Literature*, 49(1): 3–71. Refer to Table 6 of Atkinson, et al. (2011) for the reported numbers for Singapore and the comparator countries.

[19]See *ibid.*, Figure 11.

strand of this theory sees powerful lobbies seeking to influence the extent of financial regulation and tax rates that are set for high-income earners.[20]

Economic forces worked towards raising the earnings of the less skilled by more than it did the more skilled up to about the year 2000. In recognition of the economic forces turning against low-wage workers, the Singapore Workfare Income Supplement scheme was implemented in 2007. This scheme may have to be further tweaked in future, such as lowering the minimum age for qualifying, as wage inequalities are likely to continue to widen and possibly affect a wider spectrum of workers. Nevertheless, its basic design, which is to give income supplements to workers engaged in productive activities in the economy, is fundamentally sound. A well-functioning economy requires its participants to recognise that each plays a role in facilitating specialisation according to one's comparative advantage. Those who are well rewarded by the market should recognise that their high wage earnings come in part from social collaboration and so should be willing to pay higher taxes to finance wage and training subsidies for low-wage workers and those made redundant by changes in market opportunities.

---

[20]See Larry M. Bartels, 2008, *Unequal Democracy: The Political Economy of the New Gilded Age*, New York: Russell Sage Foundation and Princeton: Princeton University Press.

Chapter 2

What We Can Learn From the Data

As we saw in Figure 0.1 in the introductory chapter, Singapore's real GDP per capita, which had been growing at a pace to just maintain its relative distance to the U.S. economy, began to speed up to race towards the standard of living of the world's economic leader of the 20th century after independence in 1965. What *caused* this economic catch up and what mechanisms shape the future trajectory are critical questions we seek to answer. In order to make progress in our understanding, we need to gather data of economic variables and seek to provide a theory to organise the way we think about how these economic variables are related to each other.[1] In this chapter, we explore data to make empirical observations about the Singapore economy. Various time series of economic variables show the very large extent to which Singapore is integrated with the global economy, suggesting that Singapore's economic openness plays a causal role in the economic take-off. Another set of data provides measures of economic outcomes: real wages of workers of different levels of skill, unemployment rate, labour market tightness, and retrenchment rate. Concomitant with the changes of these economic variables over time, the measures of wealth, educational attainment, and total fertility rate have also evolved, providing clues to the future challenges facing the economy. We also make observations about the variables that show the shifts in the structure of the economy as well as the availability of fiscal resources and their uses. An examination

---

[1] See John R. Hicks, 1979, *Causality in Economics*, London: Basil Blackwell.

of past challenges and the policy responses provides insights into the workings of the Singapore economy and the way forward.

Empirical Observations

Empirical observation 1: The economy achieved an economic take-off after independence in 1965.

Figure 2.1 shows that after the Second World War, both France and Germany experienced a trajectory of an economic catch-up that is very similar to what Singapore experienced after independence. On the other hand, the U.K. continued to grow at about the rate at which the U.S. economy was growing. The war destroyed much capital in the two European Continental economies, causing an abrupt drop in their real GDP per capita. Since economic institutions were left largely intact, the rebuilding of the economies brought rapid growth in the 1950s and 1960s. The post-war investments embodied new technologies as France and Germany were able to race towards the technological frontier determined by the U.S. economy.

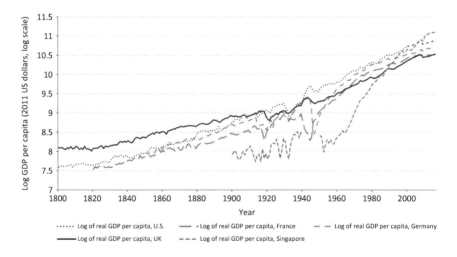

Figure 2.1:   A Longer Historical Perspective on Singapore's Catch-up Growth

Source: Maddison Project Database, version 2018. Jutta Bolt, Robert Inklaar, Herman de Jong and Jan Luiten van Zanden, 2018, "Rebasing 'Maddison': New Income Comparisons and the Shape of Long-run Economic Development," Maddison Project Working Paper, nr. 10.

The narrative of Singapore's economic development is that, through the Economic Development Board, the country adopted a strategy to attract multinational corporations to produce in Singapore for export into overseas markets.[2] With wage rates rising in the advanced economies, there were opportunities for Singapore in the 1960s to develop its economic institutions to attract these foreign firms to take advantage of a ready pool of hardworking employees at lower cost. The business-friendly environment encouraged the inflow of foreign direct investments, enabling the country to overcome financial frictions that prevented local firms from operating at a sufficiently large scale in the manufacturing sector. The multinational corporations also brought in imported technology and ready markets to sell their manufactured products into.

Noting that with a log scale, the slope of each line reflects the growth rate of the real GDP per capita, Figure 2.1 shows that Singapore grew faster than the other developed economies during the catch-up phase. Having surpassed the real GDP per capita of these economies, its growth rate has started to slow down just as France and Germany grew more slowly after their catch-up following the Second World War. While it must continue to import technologies from abroad, Singapore's further growth will be fueled by indigenous innovation.

Empirical observation 2: The share of Singapore's total trade as a ratio to GDP, already comparatively high at independence, steadily increased further. The stock of foreign direct investment as a ratio to GDP also increased. The total stock of foreign direct investment grew faster than total labour force size grew so the stock of foreign direct investment per worker has been steadily rising.

Figure 2.2 shows that the total exports plus imports as a share of GDP grew from over 200 percent in 1965 to nearly 400 percent in 2012. Figure 2.3 shows that the total stock of foreign direct investment (FDI) as a ratio to GDP increased from 0.5 in 1978 to above 2 in 2013. The strategy to attract foreign direct investments

---

[2]See Chin Bock Chan, et al., 2002, *Heart Work*, Singapore: Singapore Economic Development Board.

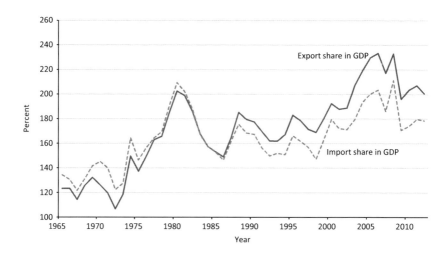

Figure 2.2:   Singapore's Economic Openness by Trade Measure, 1965–2012
Source: *Yearbook of Statistics Singapore*, various issues, Department of Statistics, Singapore.

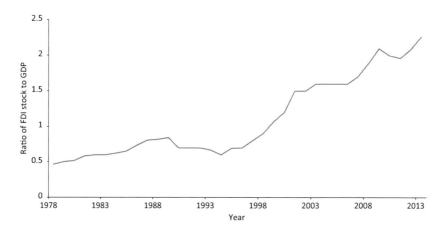

Figure 2.3:   Singapore's Economic Openness by FDI Measure, 1978–2013
Source: *Yearbook of Statistics Singapore*, various issues, Department of Statistics, Singapore.

to achieve the economic take-off is related to the rise in the trade to GDP ratio. This is because the multinational corporations in Singapore produced goods to sell into the export market. Much of the production took the form of contributing value added to imported

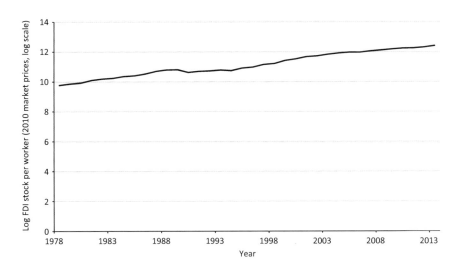

Figure 2.4: Singapore's FDI Stock per Worker, 1978–2013

Source: Yearbook of Statistics Singapore, various years, Department of Statistics, Singapore.

intermediate goods that were then re-exported. As the total stock of foreign direct investment increased faster than the growth in total labour force size, the stock of foreign direct investment per worker showed a steady increase in Figure 2.4. In other words, foreign capital grew to match the increase in the foreign workforce employed in Singapore. Attracting multinational corporations to Singapore will remain an important strategy even as the country creates an economic culture supportive of indigenous innovation by startups as well as small and medium-sized enterprises. While small and medium-sized enterprises have a tough time competing with large firms, those that eventually survive the competition grow faster than large firms and thus drive productivity and contribute to overall growth. Nevertheless, multinational corporations in general are still more productive and offer better pay compared to small and medium-sized enterprises.

Empirical observation 3: Real wages increased across the skills distribution with relatively bigger gains for the middle-skill and low-skill workers until around 2000. After that, the real wage for the middle-skill workers was somewhat flat, the real wage for the

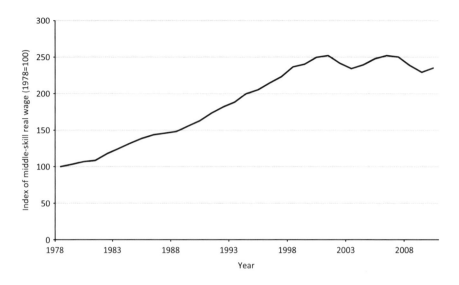

Figure 2.5:   Singapore's Middle-skill Real Wage, 1978–2010

Source: Department of Statistics, Singapore and Singapore Ministry of Manpower.

Note: Middle-skill real wage is the weighted average monthly earnings of clerical, sales, service and related workers deflated by Consumer Price Index.

high-skill workers grew more slowly while the real wage for low-skill workers declined.

Figure 2.5 shows the time series of real wage earnings for middle-skill workers, Figure 2.6 for low-skill workers, and Figure 2.7 for high-skill workers.[3] They show that wage gains were widely shared across the skills distribution until around 2000. As the inflow of foreign direct investments facilitated technological diffusion from abroad, the increased demand for workers translated into real wage gains for all workers. As Singapore's comparative advantage in earlier decades were in relatively less-skilled-labour-intensive goods, Figure 2.8 shows that middle-skill wages gained ground relative to high-skill wages until around 2000. Figure 2.9 shows the U-shaped

---

[3]The middle-skill, correspondingly middle-wage, workers include clerical, sales, service and related workers. The low-skill, correspondingly low-wage, workers include production, transport and other manual workers. The high-skill, correspondingly high-wage, workers include professional, technical, administrative, managerial, executive and related workers.

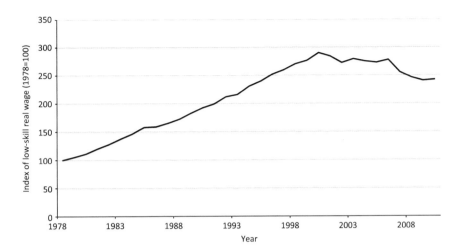

Figure 2.6: Singapore's Low-skill Real Wage, 1978–2010

Source: Department of Statistics, Singapore and Singapore Ministry of Manpower.

Note: Low-skill real wage is the weighted average monthly earnings of production, transport and other manual workers deflated by Consumer Price Index.

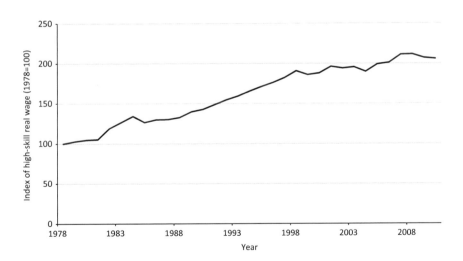

Figure 2.7: Singapore's High-skill Real Wage, 1978–2010

Source: Singapore Department of Statistics and Singapore Ministry of Manpower.

Note: High-skill real wage is the weighted average monthly earnings of professional, administrative, managerial and executive workers deflated by Consumer Price Index.

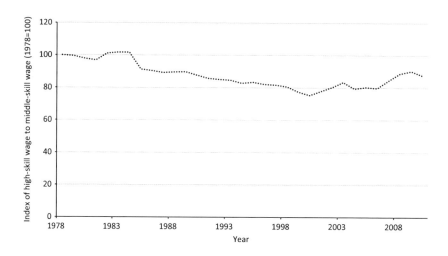

Figure 2.8: Index of High-skill Wage to Middle-skill Wage, 1978–2010
Source: Department of Statistics, Singapore and Singapore Ministry of Manpower.
Note: The ratio of high-skill wage to middle-skill wage in 1978 is 2.95.

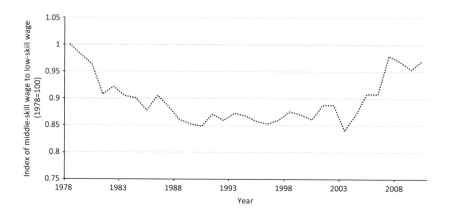

Figure 2.9: Index of Middle-skill Wage to Low-skill Wage, 1978–2010
Source: Department of Statistics, Singapore and Singapore Ministry of Manpower.
Note: The ratio of middle-skill wage to low-skill wage in 1978 is 1.23.

pattern for relative earnings of middle-skill relative to low-skill workers similar to the U-shaped pattern seen previously in Chapter 1 (Figure 1.4) for relative earnings of high-skill to low-skill workers. Until around 2000, therefore, economic growth occurred with a narrowing wage gap — the gap between the high-skill and middle-skill, that between the middle-skill and low-skill, as well as the gap between the high-skill and low-skill. The first decade of the new millennium saw stagnant wage earnings for middle-skill workers, wage declines for low skill workers, and moderate wage growth for high-skill workers. This can be explained as follows. The first half of the 2000s saw Singapore experience several recessionary shocks — the September 11 attacks in the U.S., the end of the internet boom, and the flu epidemic — which had a wage dampening effect on all workers. In addition, shifts in comparative advantage towards relatively more skilled-labour-intensive goods and the onslaught of skill-biased-technological progress acted to widen the wage gap, benefitting workers with higher skill and depressing earnings of low-wage workers. As Singapore moves higher up on the value chain, it is the demand for more-skilled workers that increases, which pulls up their wage earnings. With the widespread use of computers in production, there is a further premium placed on workers' skills. The arrival of artificial intelligence, machine learning, and robotics makes possible the substitution of certain tasks previously performed by workers and thus depresses wages. On the other hand, it is likely that new tasks will also be created that human workers have a comparative advantage in performing. This creates labour demand and pulls up wages. A preparation of the workforce to acquire the skills to perform these new tasks will provide engaging jobs with good pay.

Empirical observation 4: There was a fairly steady decline in the unemployment rate with relatively stable inflation after 1965. During recessionary episodes when the unemployment rate jumped up, policy measures to lower unit labour costs were adopted to save jobs.

Figure 2.10 plots the unemployment rate along with the inflation rate. Figure 2.11 presents a long time series plot of French unemployment rate juxtaposed against Singapore's unemployment rate. The French unemployment rate was very low in the 1960s but began a steady climb to reach a level above 8 percent by the 1980s. The

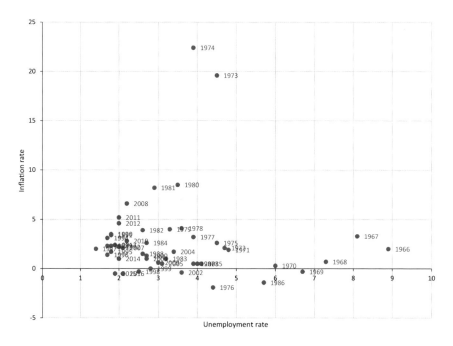

Figure 2.10:   Inflation-Unemployment Relationship, 1966–2016

Source: *Yearbook of Statistics Singapore*, various years, Department of Statistics, Singapore.

two decades of post-war rebuilding saw the French economy enjoy low unemployment rates. The cause of its subsequent steady rise through the 1970s and 1980s, a phenomenon that has also occurred in several of the other European economies, has been a subject of research. The economist Stephen Nickell has argued that a shift in labour market institutions, which include the unemployment benefit system, employment protection legislation, and the system of wage determination, is a major explanatory factor.[4] The present author

---

[4] See Stephen Nickell, Luca Nunziata and Wolfgang Ochel, 2005, "Unemployment in the OECD Since the 1960s. What Do We Know?" *Economic Journal*, 115(500): 1–27. The paper found that having more generous unemployment benefit systems and stronger employment legislation, which make it more costly for firms to dismiss workers, have positive effects on unemployment. An increase in trade union pressure to raise wages is also found to raise unemployment.

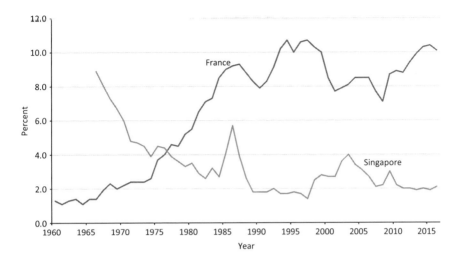

Figure 2.11: Unemployment Rate for France and Singapore

Source: Federal Reserve Bank of St. Louis and *Yearbook of Statistics Singapore*, various years, Department of Statistics, Singapore.

and the economist Edmund Phelps have argued that a decline in productivity growth is a contributory factor in the rise of European unemployment from the late seventies.[5] Meanwhile, Singapore's unemployment rate steadily declined as its catch-up growth increased the real wage that firms could afford to pay and yet remain profitable. The slowdown in growth as the Singapore economy gets closer to the technology frontier will slow down the growth of firms' affordable wage. If workers' wage aspirations do not adjust to this slowdown, then the rate of unemployment will rise. The nature of labour market institutions that evolve to cope with the new realities will also have an impact on the unemployment rate.

Figure 2.12 shows very high values of the measure of labour market tightness represented by the number of job vacancies per unemployed worker in the decade before the Asian financial crisis but which dropped to around 0.5 during the recessions in 1998, 2003 and

---

[5]Hian Teck Hoon and Edmund S. Phelps, 1997, "Growth, Wealth and the Natural Rate of Unemployment: Is Europe's Jobs Crisis a Growth Crisis?" *European Economic Review: Papers and Proceedings*, 41(3–5): 549–557.

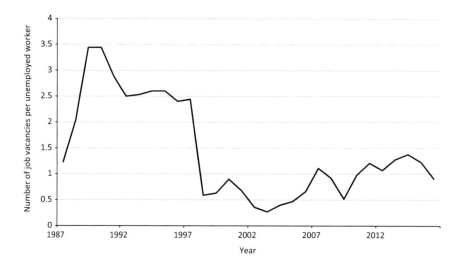

Figure 2.12:   Singapore's Labour Market Tightness, 1987–2016

Source: *Singapore Yearbook of Manpower Statistics*, various years and Singapore Ministry of Manpower.

Note: Measure of labour market tightness is computed by taking the ratio of vacancy rate to annual average unemployment rate from 1987 to 2016.

2009. Figure 2.13 shows upward jumps in the rate of retrenchment during these recessionary years. Cost-cutting measures such as cuts in employers' Central Provident Fund contributions and the use of wage subsidies as a means to fight recessions resulted in the variation of unit labour costs as shown in Figure 2.14. By lowering the unit cost of production, wage subsidies enabled firms to hold on to their workers and not lay them off during recessions. With technological advances and automation, certain jobs, particularly those which are of a routine nature, may be replaced. However, new types of jobs will also be created. To prevent unemployment resulting from skills mismatch, the workforce would have to continuously upgrade their skills.

Empirical observation 5: Consumption share of aggregate demand has declined while the investment share and share of net exports have increased. The latter two time series show greater volatility.

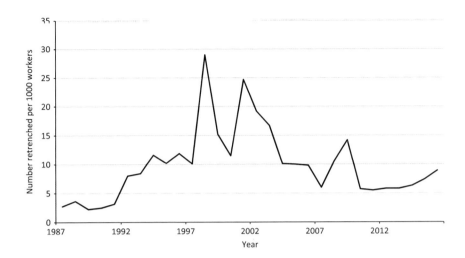

Figure 2.13:   Singapore's Retrenchment Rate, 1987–2016
Source: *Singapore Yearbook of Manpower Statistics*, various years.

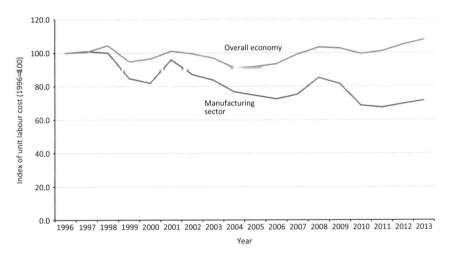

Figure 2.14:   Unit Labour Cost for Manufacturing and Overall Economy, 1996–2013
Source: *Yearbook of Statistics Singapore*, various years, Department of Statistics, Singapore.

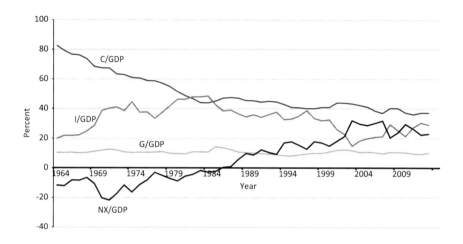

Figure 2.15:   Composition of Aggregate Demand over time, 1964–2013

Source: *Yearbook of Statistics Singapore*, various years, Department of Statistics, Singapore.

Note: C/GDP is consumption share of GDP; I/GDP is investment share of GDP; G/GDP is government expenditure share of GDP; NX/GDP is net exports share of GDP.

Figure 2.15 shows the change in the composition of aggregate demand over time. Consumption, which made up about 80 percent of GDP in 1965, steadily declined to reach about 40 percent in the present decade. As the value of imports of goods and services exceeded the value of exports, Singapore ran a trade deficit until the mid-1980s. Since then, it has run a trade surplus with net exports continuing to grow, exceeding 20 percent of GDP by the early 2000s.[6] With a greater reliance on the external market, developments in the global economy now exert a bigger impact on Singapore's GDP. Economic downturns and recoveries in the advanced economies cause greater volatility in the domestic economy. Total investment, also called gross fixed capital formation, as a share of GDP was double

---

[6]A more detailed analysis shows that Singapore has been running a small trade deficit in services so that the overall trade surplus is due to a growing trade surplus in merchandise or goods that exceeds the services deficit. See Singapore Ministry of Trade and Industry, 2016, "Trends in Singapore's International Trade in Services," *Statistics Singapore Newsletter*, March.

that of the U.S. in the 1970s and 1980s but has declined in the 2000s to levels more similar to the U.S. Foreign direct investment has played an important role in economic recovery as its share in total investment increased, especially in the years after the global financial crisis caused Singapore to enter a recession in 2009. Expansionary fiscal policy taking the form of an increase in public investment has also served to help in economic recovery when the economy was buffeted by recessionary shocks.

Empirical observation 6: With a relatively high national savings rate, net wealth per capita steadily increased.

Figure 2.16 shows the evolution of the national savings as a ratio to gross national income along with the investment as a ratio to gross national income. As total investment exceeded national savings, the current account was in deficit until the mid-1980s. Since then, national savings has exceeded total investment so the current

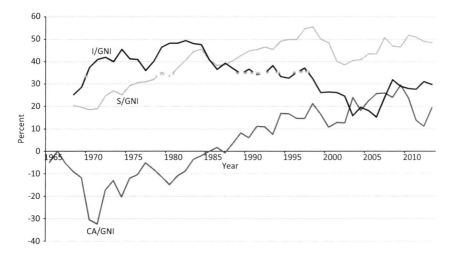

Figure 2.16: National Savings and Investment Share of Gross National Income, 1965–2013

Source: *Yearbook of Statistics Singapore*, various years, Department of Statistics, Singapore.

Note: S/GNI is national savings share of gross national income; I/GNI is investment share of gross national income; CA/GNI is current account share of gross national income.

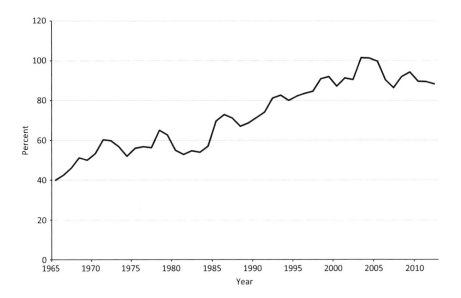

Figure 2.17:   Stock of Official Foreign Reserves relative to GDP, 1965–2012

Source: *Yearbook of Statistics Singapore*, various years, Department of Statistics, Singapore.

account has been in surplus. The accumulation of net foreign assets is reflected in Figure 2.17 showing a steady rise in the stock of foreign reserves as a share of GDP over time.[7] The increase in the stock of foreign reserves provides the country with assets that can be drawn upon to fight recessions. This occurred in 2009 when a wage subsidy called Jobs Credit was given to businesses to encourage them not to lay off Singaporean workers. Jobs Credit was financed by drawing from Singapore's reserves, and the money was returned in 2011 after an economic recovery.

---

[7]Private wealth, as measured by the net worth of the household sector, taken as a ratio to GDP also increased from below 350 percent in 2000 to nearly 400 percent in 2016. Net worth is equal to household assets minus household liabilities; the former includes currency and deposits, shares and securities, life insurance, CPF balances, pension funds, and private and public residential property, while the latter includes mortgages and personal loans (for example, motor vehicle loans, credit card loans, and other personal loans from banks and other financial institutions). Source: Department of Statistics, Singapore Ministry of Trade and Industry, *Yearbook of Statistics Singapore, 2017*.

How would wealth and productivity growth affect Singapore's future employment prospects? A slowdown in productivity growth acts to reduce workers' real wage relative to the sum of private and national wealth, which can blunt workers' incentive to supply effort and encourage greater labour turnover. The need to motivate workers and reduce labour turnover by paying employees more leads to higher costs of production, with the consequence that firms cut down total employment. As each firm cuts down its employed workforce, the economy's rate of unemployment is pushed up. The greater difficulty in finding a job should a worker quit or be dismissed due to malfeasance, acts to limit labour turnover and to motivate the supply of work effort.

Empirical observation 7: The average number of years of schooling has steadily increased since 1950. The share of the population with tertiary education saw big increases after 1990.

Figure 2.18 shows the index of human capital rising from 1950. Figure 2.19 shows that the percentage of the population aged 15 and above with tertiary education saw big increases after 1990. Human capital accumulation directly contributes another source of GDP growth on top of physical capital accumulation. In addition, the larger stock of human capital itself enables Singapore to better

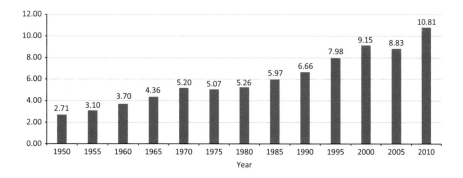

Figure 2.18: Singapore's Average Years of Total Schooling since 1950

Source: Robert Barro and Jong-Wha Lee, 2013, "A New Data Set of Educational Attainment in the World, 1950–2010," *Journal of Development Economics*, 104 (September): 184–198.

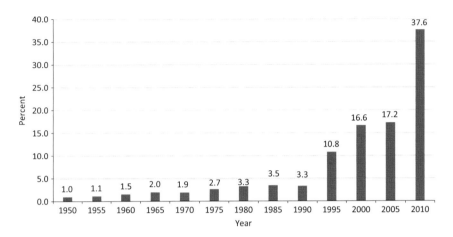

Figure 2.19:   Percentage of Population aged 15 and over with Tertiary Education since 1950

Source: Robert Barro and Jong-Wha Lee, 2013, "A New Data Set of Educational Attainment in the World, 1950–2010," *Journal of Development Economics*, 104 (September): 184–198.

absorb technology from abroad thus facilitating technological diffusion. With the arrival of a general purpose technology taking the form of digitisation, a more educated workforce is better able to cope with new applications of digital technology. More of them might be willing to launch business startups, taking advantage of digitisation to reach customers in overseas markets. Along with a growing share of the workforce having tertiary education comes a higher demand for high-skill jobs as job preferences shift. It will be necessary for the economy of the future to create the jobs desired by high-skill workers. Such jobs could involve new tasks that are created to harness the possibilities brought about by artificial intelligence and robotics.

Empirical observation 8: Total fertility rate shows a steady decline and fell to below replacement level by the mid-1970s.

Figure 2.20 shows the total fertility rate decline from above 5 in 1960 to around replacement level by the mid-1970s and it continued to decline to 1.2 in 2016. The decline in the total fertility rate as a country becomes richer appears to be a fairly general phenomenon. As people become richer, they choose to have fewer

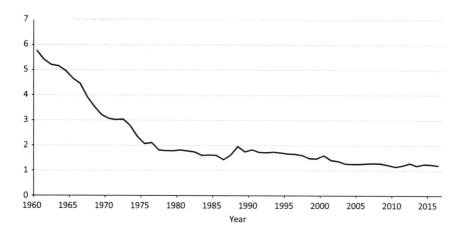

Figure 2.20: Singapore's Total Fertility Rate, 1960–2016
Source: Department of Statistics, Singapore.

children but make heavy investment in their children's education. Given the past trend of total fertility rate, the growth of Singapore's citizen workforce will slow from now to 2020 and its size is expected to decline thereafter.[8] If innovation requires creative and talented people, and if the probability of being a creative and talented person is independently distributed among people, then it follows that a greater number of creative and talented people would be found within a larger population. If it is people who create ideas, then a decline in total fertility rate means a shrinking workforce, which is likely to reduce the flow of innovative ideas.

Empirical observation 9: The manufacturing sector has declined as a share of total GDP as well as a share of total resident employment, giving way to the bigger share occupied by the services sector. Manufacturing share of the stock of foreign direct investment has also declined.

Figure 2.21 shows the manufacturing share of total GDP increase from about 15 percent in 1965 to nearly 30 percent by the early

---

[8]See Singapore Ministry of Manpower, Annex to Statement on Labour Market Developments (March 2015).

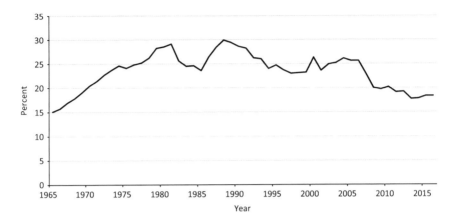

Figure 2.21:   Share of Manufacturing in GDP at Current Market Prices, 1965–2016

Source: *Yearbook of Statistics Singapore*, various years, Department of Statistics, Singapore.

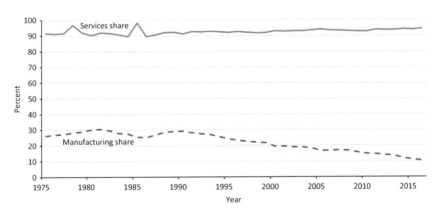

Figure 2.22:   Manufacturing and Services Share of Total Resident Employment, 1975–2016

Source: *Yearbook of Statistics Singapore*, various issues, Department of Statistics, Singapore.

1980s, but it has been declining since the late eighties to hover around 20 percent today. While the manufacturing sector's share of total GDP has stayed around 20 percent, Figure 2.22 shows that its share of total resident employment has been on a steady decline since

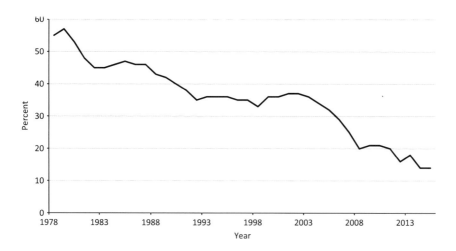

Figure 2.23: Manufacturing Share of Total FDI Stock, 1978–2015

Source: Yearbook of Statistics Singapore, various issues, Department of Statistics, Singapore.

around 1990. The services sector share of total resident employment has increased as the manufacturing share has declined. The relative expansion of the employment share of the services sector can in part be explained by the fact that the services sector is relatively more labour-intensive compared to the manufacturing sector. As the economy accumulates more capital, and as productivity growth in the manufacturing sector outpaces that of the services sector, labour is released from the manufacturing sector to work in the services sector. Figure 2.23 shows the decline in manufacturing's share of total stock of foreign direct investment. The decline has been particularly more pronounced since 2003 as the foreign direct investment has flowed into the services sector. This is encouraging insofar as the shift of the labour force towards employment in the services sector is accompanied by a concomitant increase in capital employed there. The accompanying rise in capital stock helps to hold up the productivity of workers in the services sector. The growth in the relative size of the services sector also means that this sector plays an increasingly larger role in supporting the indigenous innovation necessary for economic prosperity in the next phase of growth.

Empirical observation 10: Tax revenue has grown in tandem with the expanding GDP thus providing adequate resources to finance total government spending. Income taxes provide the biggest share of total tax revenue. Social spending as a ratio to total government expenditure has shown a trend increase.

Figure 2.24 shows that with a fairly stable share of tax revenue out of GDP, the growth in tax revenue has been adequate to finance government spending, generating budgetary surpluses in most years. Figure 2.25 shows that income taxes make up the biggest share of total tax revenue.[9] Customs and excise duties have undergone a steady decline as a contributor to total tax revenue. On the government expenditure side, Figure 2.26 shows that social spending as a share of total government expenditure has increased over time. With an expected increase in healthcare spending as the population ages and as various forces act to widen wage inequality, the future challenge is to generate enough tax revenue to finance social spending

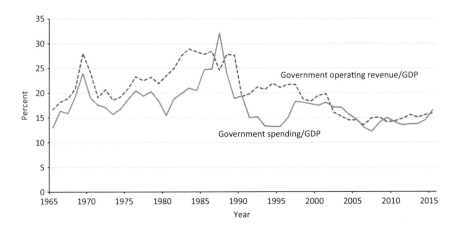

Figure 2.24: Government Spending and Tax Revenue Relative to GDP, 1965–2015

Source: *Yearbook of Statistics Singapore*, various years, Department of Statistics, Singapore.

---

[9]Income taxes are made up of corporate income tax, personal income tax, and withholding tax, with corporate tax making up more than half of the total in recent years.

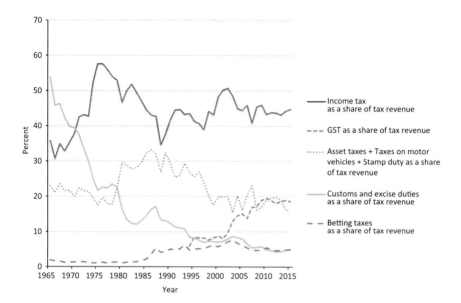

Figure 2.25: Composition of Tax Revenue, 1965–2015

Source: *Yearbook of Statistics Singapore*, various years, Deparment of Statistics, Singapore.

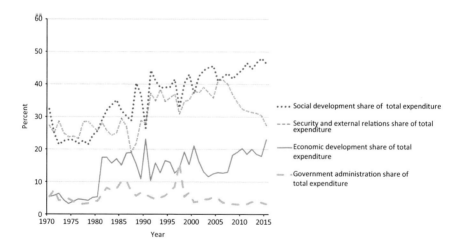

Figure 2.26: Composition of Government Spending, 1970–2015

Source: *Yearbook of Statistics Singapore*, various issues, Department of Statistics, Singapore.

and achieve economic inclusion. A shrinking workforce contracts the tax base directly by reducing GDP at given productivity and indirectly by slowing the pace of innovation (if the flow of innovative ideas is proportional to the size of the workforce). To sustain a steady flow of fiscal resources to finance social spending, it is necessary to keep the labour force size from shrinking through a two-prong policy to boost total fertility and manage a controlled inflow of immigrants.

Past Challenges and Policy Responses

Prior to its independence in 1965, Singapore's real GDP per capita maintained a steady gap with the frontier economies of France, Germany, the United Kingdom, and the United States. It was a relatively poor country growing at the frontier economies' trend growth rate. The question after independence was how to achieve an economic take-off. The answer is that the choice to remain integrated with the global economy and to attract foreign direct investments facilitated technological diffusion from the frontier economies, overcoming the constraints faced by local firms to raise finance to meet the minimum scale of operation. The multinational corporations that set up their factories in Singapore produced parts and components as well as final goods whose technology contents were previously developed in the frontier economies. These multinational corporations, as well as local sub-contractors, also imported capital goods embodying existing technology to use as intermediate products to produce goods further up the value chain. Growing trade integration brought in technologies developed in the frontier economies through capital good imports, and the setting up of multinational corporations also brought new management practices to the workplace. Being more productive, the multinational corporations could readily pay the fixed cost of setting up export platforms to sell into the global economy, so total exports as a share GDP also grew. With a large technology gap initially, Singapore could benefit from the advantages of relative economic backwardness. As a result, Singapore started to grow faster than the frontier economies during a phase of catch-up growth.

The size of the total labour force grew six-fold from 0.58 million workers in 1966 to 3.44 million in 2014. However, even as the size of the total workforce grew when the baby boom generation entered the workforce and the inflow of foreign workers increased, the inflow of foreign direct investment grew even more so the stock of foreign direct investment per worker steadily increased. New jobs were created at an even faster pace than labour force growth so that the average annual rate of unemployment steadily declined. At the same time, real wage gains were enjoyed by all segments of the workforce at least until 2000. An important question is how the economy managed workers' wage aspirations without rising unemployment. In Hoon (2006), I identified two periods, the Catch-up phase (1966–1985) and the Golden Decade (1989–1998), that are instructive for thinking about how the economy managed this.[10] During the catch-up phase, it is likely that technological diffusion from the frontier economies led to growth that far exceeded workers' expectations. The technological diffusion raised the marginal revenue product of labour and thus the affordable wage that firms could pay while remaining profitable even as workers' required wage grew only modestly.[11] The consequence is that the labour market tightened, the unemployment rate declined, and real wages increased.[12] During the Golden Decade, while the

---

[10]The full citation is Hian Teck Hoon, 2006, "Future Job Prospects in Singapore," in Winston T. H. Koh and Roberto S. Mariano (eds.) *Economic Prospects of Singapore*, Singapore: Addison-Wesley, pp. 47–78. A working paper version can be downloaded by going to my homepage https://sites.google.com/site/hthoon/ and using the hyperlink to *Institutional Knowledge at Singapore Management University.*

[11]A worker's required wage is the wage that a worker bargains for in order to keep him or her happy enough to remain with his or her current employer. This required wage is higher the tighter is the labour market and is also higher, at any given level of labour market tightness, the stronger is the wage aspiration. It can be argued that the wage aspiration is positively related to workers' forecasts of future productivity growth. The more optimistic they are about future productivity growth, the stronger is their wage aspiration. What matters for unemployment rate determination, holding everything else constant, is the gap between the forecast of productivity growth and the actual productivity growth achieved.

[12]During the catch-up phase, actual productivity growth very likely exceeded forecasted productivity growth.

unemployment rate remained steady at about 2 percent and real wages continued to rise, the measure of labour market tightness given by the number of job vacancies per unemployed worker, actually declined. Using the search-matching framework, the explanation I offered for why the unemployment rate could remain so low when the level of labour-market tightness was declining is that the Beveridge curve (giving a negative relationship between the job vacancy rate and the unemployment rate) shifted due to improved matching between workers and vacant job slots. The Golden Decade coincided with two events: first, a booming regional economy that led to a thriving financial sector as funds flowed into the region and, second, the start of the telecommunications and internet boom. Singapore had a ready supply of the financial sector workers as well as IT-trained workers needed to fill many new job vacancies that were created as a result of these two events. Consequently, job matching was relatively easy, implying an inward shift of the Beveridge curve.[13]

While choosing to be integrated into the global economy to catch waves of opportunities, the Singapore economy was invariably subject also to negative external shocks such as the shock emanating from the Asian financial crisis in 1998, the shock from the September 2001 terrorist attack in New York as well as the shock from the global financial crisis in 2009. What policy measures were adopted to attenuate these negative external shocks? Since 1981, the Monetary Authority of Singapore has adopted an exchange-rate-based policy rule to adjust the exchange rate against a basket of currencies according to how far the inflation rate has deviated from an implicit inflation target and the size of the output gap.[14] Thus, the exchange rate would be weakened during these recessionary episodes following the policy rule. In addition to the exchange-rate

---

[13]My hypothesis is that, in the absence of the improved matching between workers with the necessary skills (IT and finance skills) and the required job tasks, the slower actual (compared to forecasted) productivity growth would have raised the unemployment rate.

[14]The output gap measures how far actual GDP falls below the estimated potential output.

adjustment, however, extra measures were adopted to cut unit labour costs in the form of cuts in employers' Central Provident Fund contributions and, in 2009, wage subsidies (also called jobs credits) funded by the government.[15] Notably during the global financial crisis of 2009, the government funded the jobs credits by drawing down its reserves accumulated from fiscal surpluses during the years of economic expansion.[16] A spike in the jobs separation rate both shifts out the Beveridge curve, implying a higher unemployment rate at a given vacancy rate, and downward shifts of the labour demand curve as firms reduce the number of job vacancies per unemployed worker at a given wage rate. A jobs credit increases the surplus that a firm can enjoy from a successful job match, thus attenuating the tendency to reduce hiring during economic downturns.[17]

The export of relatively less-skilled-labour-intensive goods into the global market helped to pull up the wage earnings of low-skill workers relative to the wage earnings of the high-skill and middle-skill workers. The shift in comparative advantage out of less-skilled-labour-intensive goods into higher-skilled-labour-intensive goods and the onslaught of skill-biased technology brought this period of narrowing wage gaps in favour of low-skill workers to an end by 2000. During the period I identified as the Turbulent Years (1998–2003) that began with the Asian financial crisis, the period of steady growth in real wage earnings ended. However, while the real wage earnings of middle-skill workers stagnated and the real wage earnings of high-skill workers saw anaemic growth, the real wage earnings of low-skill workers saw an absolute decline. In response, the government introduced as a permanent pillar of the social safety net system a wage income supplement scheme, formally called the Workfare

---

[15] See Hian Teck Hoon, 2014, "Wage Subsidies as a Tool to Fight Recessions," in *Macroeconomic Review*, Volume XIII, Issue 2: 91–96 published by the Economic Policy Group, Monetary Authority of Singapore.

[16] After the storm was over, the government returned the reserves it drew earlier to fund the jobs credits.

[17] A jobs credit helps to attenuate the downward shift of the labour demand curve.

Income Supplement scheme, which raised the take-home pay of low-wage workers.[18]

In summary, when faced with the challenge of how to achieve an economic take-off after independence, Singapore chose to become more integrated into the global economy. Its policy of welcoming foreign direct investments enabled the country to overcome the financial constraints that had prevented local firms from undertaking investment in the manufacturing sector, as many activities in that sector required a minimum scale. The entry of multinational corporations facilitated technological diffusion from the frontier economies, gradually closing the technology gap as the economy grew faster than the frontier economies in order to catch up. Tackling the challenge of managing workers' wage aspirations without rising unemployment relied first on delivering growth that exceeded workers' expectations during the catch-up phase. During this phase, the wage that firms could afford to pay ran ahead of workers' required wage needed to keep them in their jobs so the unemployment rate steadily declined even as real wages rose. Later, the ability to supply workers with the necessary skills to catch the waves of opportunity brought by capital inflows into the region, and the start of the communications and internet boom, improved employer-worker matches. Improved job matching kept the unemployment rate low even as the measure of labour market tightness declined and real wages continued to increase. During the years of exceptional growth, fiscal prudence led to the accumulation of reserves that provided the resources to finance

---

[18]A wage income supplement given directly to workers has the effect of driving a wedge between the firm's affordable wage and the worker's required wage and acts to increase the measure of labour market tightness. As a consequence, not only is the low-wage worker's take-home pay increased, the employment rate of low-wage workers is also increased. A study by economists at Singapore Ministry of Trade and Industry found, using a difference-in-differences estimation strategy to analyse data from 2007 to 2010, that the introduction of the Workfare Income Supplement scheme gave incentives to less-educated Singaporeans, particularly those in the older age groups, to enter and stay in the workforce. See the feature article titled "The impact of the Workfare Income Supplement scheme on individuals' labour outcomes" in *Economic Survey of Singapore Second Quarter 2014*, Singapore Ministry of Trade and Industry.

wage subsidies to save jobs in 2009 when the economy was faced with challenges coming from negative external shocks. When comparative advantage shifted away from less-skilled-labour-intensive goods and new technologies were skill-biased, the real wages of low-skill workers experienced absolute declines turning an initial period of narrowing wage gaps to widening wage gaps after 2000. In response, fiscal resources were drawn upon to finance wage income supplements given to low-wage workers from 2007 through the Workfare Income Supplement scheme.

Going Forward

Going forward, Singapore would have to find the social consensus and political support to embrace economic openness in order to generate resources to support schemes that foster economic inclusion, such as the Workfare Income Supplement scheme. With the digital revolution destroying jobs that perform routine tasks, resources are also required to finance employment and training subsidies given to firms to encourage them to hire and train displaced workers. While the end of the catch-up phase brings slower growth compared to the past, Singapore can still obtain further growth in living standards by generating productivity growth from indigenous innovation and applications of frontier technology. Since in any given industry, there is a distribution of firms with different levels of productivity, there is greater scope to generate indigenous innovation by finding means to boost the productivity of firms — both new startups as well as existing firms — at the left tail of the distribution. This can occur with the adoption of good management practices, development of new unique products, and entry into overseas markets. As industry-level trade missions into the regional economies gather useful information that each firm can take advantage of to expand sales, there are external economies of scale that benefit each firm. The higher human capital stock reflected in the increase in the share of the population with tertiary education means a workforce that is more prepared to navigate the unfamiliar terrain brought about by the digital revolution. Digitisation also enables more firms to sell in export markets. As export-oriented firms are larger, they can devote more resources to screen workers and improve the quality of their workforce. As a result, they are able to pay higher wages.

The successful matching of workers with the right skills to meet the needs of the new jobs in the future economy will help to keep Singapore's unemployment rate low. Stronger employment legislation to make it more expensive for firms to lay off workers when there is a business downturn has the effect of making firms more reluctant to create permanent jobs in the first place. While increasing severance costs reduces the retrenchment rate, the slower pace of job creation has the unintended consequence of prolonging the duration of unemployment when a worker does lose his job.[19] With the disruption brought about by the digital revolution, our schools will need to teach people how to learn so that they thrive in an environment fraught with novelties. In addition, while most of the new jobs would have to be created by the private sector, the government can play the role of facilitating a close communication between businesses and educational institutions so that supply can match the demand for new skills.

As new business ventures sell into the world market, this will mean facing adverse external shocks from time to time. In order to finance jobs credits during episodes of negative external shocks, the government would need to run budget surpluses during good times. Even though the phase of catch-up growth is over, Singapore can learn from mature economies that there are episodes when economic activity picks up such as during the U.S. internet boom in the late nineties. During such booms, tax revenues increase as the tax base expands at unchanged tax rates. A fiscally prudent government will save up these additional fiscal resources in order to use them to

---

[19]The economist Jean Tirole has noted that strong employment legislation in France has led firms to create temporary or short-term contract jobs rather than permanent jobs. Paradoxically, this has increased the job insecurity of both workers on temporary contracts, who have to think about how to get their next job as their contract ends, as well as workers on permanent contracts who fear that it would become very difficult to land another permanent job should they ever lose their current job. See Jean Tirole, 2017, *Economics for the Common Good*, Princeton: Princeton University Press.

hasten economic recovery when the economy is hit by a recessionary shock. The tax structure also has to be designed to optimally raise the required tax revenue to achieve equity according to the social weights assigned to different members of society along the income distribution. With wage gains going disproportionately to workers at the top end of the income distribution since 2000, there is a case for an increase in top marginal tax rates.[20] The tax base needs to grow on a sustained basis to enable the government to have the fiscal resources to fund wage income supplements for low-skill workers and training subsidies for middle-skill workers.

---

[20]See Peter Diamond and Emmanuel Saez, 2011, "The Case for a Progressive Tax: From Basic Research to Policy Recommendations," *Journal of Economic Perspectives*, 25(4): 165–190.

Chapter 3

Standard of Living

Over the long term, the standard of living is raised when there is sustained economic growth. However, even when a country has started on a path of sustained growth, the upward climb in living standards is not smooth. There are periodic shocks that cause economies to enter into recessions. Thus there are also business fluctuations that affect inflation and unemployment. In this chapter our focus is on economic growth; the next chapter picks up the theme of business fluctuations.

Thinking about modern economic growth starts from the work of the economist Robert Solow who presented an aggregative model of the economy.[1] The Solow model gives a prominent role to diminishing returns to physical capital accumulation to show that, ultimately, sustained growth requires a steady increase in total factor productivity. Total factor productivity, in turn, depends on access to useful technology as well as overall efficiency in the combination of factor inputs in the production process. The catch-up to the world technology frontier after independence helped propel Singapore's economic growth. Capital accumulation also played a significant role in the phase of catch-up growth in the context of shifting comparative advantage. Human capital accumulation will play a bigger role in

---

[1]See Robert M. Solow, 1956, "A Contribution to the Theory of Economic Growth," *Quarterly Journal of Economics*, 70(1): 65–94 for the development of the theory of growth and Robert M. Solow, 1957, "Technical Change and the Aggregate Production Function," *Review of Economics and Statistics*, 39(3): 312–320 for an exercise in growth accounting applied to the U.S. economy.

propelling Singapore's future economic growth as a mature economy since a skilled workforce is better able to cope with novel applications of new technology. The complementary role played by small and medium-sized firms alongside large firms needs to be understood to generate future economic prosperity. In this chapter, we apply theory to interpret Singapore's past growth experience and analyse possible future growth paths.

Catch-up to Technology Frontier

At the centre of growth theory is the concept of an aggregate production function that links factor inputs to output or total real GDP with a given technology. In its simplest form, the two factor inputs are physical capital — machines — and labour. Doubling the stock of physical capital and labour inputs would double the quantity of output, a property of the production function which we call constant returns to scale. If technology is held constant, this property of the production function gives the result that the real GDP per capita is positively related to the number of machines per worker, that is, the physical capital-labour ratio.[2] The higher the capital-labour ratio, the greater is the capital intensity. The marginal product of capital, which is the addition to output from using one more machine, exhibits diminishing returns so that it declines as the capital intensity rises. Intuitively, as workers have more machines to work with, the average labour productivity increases but it increases at a diminishing rate. If technology is held constant, the standard of living will initially grow as capital accumulation boosts average labour productivity but it will ultimately stagnate (at a higher level) when the amount of investment undertaken is just enough to replace capital depreciation and equip each new entrant into the labour force with the same capital intensity as the existing workforce.

Observers of the remarkable growth of the East Asian economies, including Hong Kong, Singapore, South Korea, and Taiwan, from the

---

[2]More specifically, the real GDP per capita is positively related to the capital-labour ratio as well as the labour force participation rate.

1960s have pointed to the huge role played by capital accumulation in the growth process to suggest that growth of standard of living would peter out at some point due to diminishing returns. Notable among them is the work of the economist Alwyn Young who conducted a growth accounting exercise for these economies.[3] A growth accounting exercise assumes that an economy's GDP depends on factor inputs and total factor productivity (TFP) according to a certain production function. National income accountants provide estimates of the economy's GDP as well as the contributions of factor inputs in any given year. The contribution of TFP to the growth of GDP is obtained as the residual left over after the growth of factor inputs (appropriately weighted according to the weight of each factor input in the production function) is subtracted from the growth of GDP. Young applied this methodology to Singapore data, for both the overall economy as well as for the manufacturing sector alone, for the period 1966–1990. For the overall economy, he found negligible growth of TFP (0.2 percent) for 1966–1990. Quite remarkably, for the sub-periods, 1970–1980 and 1980–1990, he found negative TFP growth for the overall economy.[4] For the manufacturing sector alone, Young found TFP growth of −0.9 percent for 1970–1980 and −1,1 percent for 1980–1990.

A paper by the economist Chang-Tai Hsieh in 2002 made the observation that if the growth of GDP in the East Asian economies was largely driven by capital accumulation with a negligible role played by the growth of TFP, then the return to capital should have fallen dramatically as capital accumulation faces diminishing

---

[3]See Alwyn Young, 1995, "The Tyranny of Numbers: Confronting the Statistical Realities of the East Asian Growth Experience," *Quarterly Journal of Economics*, 110(3): 641–680. An earlier paper of Young conducted a growth accounting exercise for, and made comparisons between, Hong Kong and Singapore. See Alwyn Young, 1992, "A Tale of Two Cities: Factor Accumulation and Technical Change in Hong Kong and Singapore," in *NBER Macroeconomics Annual 1992*, Cambridge, MA: MIT Press.

[4]For the overall economy, he found TFP growth of −0.9 percent for 1970–1980 and −0.5 percent for 1980–1990. See Table VI in Young (1995) for his calculations of Singapore's TFP growth.

returns.[5] Instead of obtaining quantity-based (primal) estimates of TFP growth, which is what Young did, Hsieh computed price-based (dual) estimates of TFP growth for the same four countries that Young studied. For Singapore, Hsieh found far higher TFP growth using the price-based (dual) estimates compared to the quantity-based (primal) estimates. For example, from 1971–1990, the TFP growth was found to be 1.78 percent using the dual approach compared to −0.69 percent using the primal approach.[6] Hsieh's explanation for the discrepancy in the estimates of TFP growth using the dual and primal approaches is that the return to capital in Singapore (for the period he studied) remained constant despite the high rate of capital accumulation. He concluded that the evidence suggests that Singapore's national accounts significantly overstated the amount of investment spending.[7]

I find Hsieh's findings consistent with the strategy Singapore adopted to take off into catch-up growth after independence. The strategy was to attract multinational firms to locate in Singapore to produce for the world market, which effected technology transfer from the frontier economies. The technology brought by the multinational firms itself spurred capital accumulation so that while diminishing returns set in when holding technology constant, the steady transfer of technology provided an escape from the drag on the return to capital. The rate of growth of technology applied domestically in production processes depends negatively on the technology gap — the ratio of frontier technology and domestically applied technology. When the technology gap was huge in 1965, the availability of low-hanging fruits of technology enabled a faster pace of TFP growth. As the technology gap narrowed over the decades, the rate of TFP growth correspondingly declined. As a mature economy, Singapore's growth rate is determined by the sum of growth based on importing technologies developed abroad and that based

---

[5]See Chang-Tai Hsieh, 2002, "What Explains the Industrial Revolution in East Asia? Evidence from the Factor Markets," *American Economic Review*, 92(3): 502–526.

[6]See Table 1 in Hsieh (2002).

[7]See Hsieh (2002), p. 503.

on indigenous innovation. How close the Singapore economy will be relative to the frontier economies in its mature phase depends on how effective it is in absorbing technology from abroad. The effectiveness of technology absorption is, in turn, dependent on the importance of inward foreign direct investment and trade relative to the country's GDP. Additional growth for the Singapore economy beyond that coming from adopting best practices from the world technology frontier comes from its indigenous innovation.

It is important to note that the TFP index does not capture only technology alone. Since it is, by construction, a residual left over after the contributions of all factor inputs to GDP have been accounted for, TFP is commonly understood to capture also the overall efficiency with which the economy uses its factor inputs. Hence, TFP also captures the quality of institutions and business efficiency. Applying a technique analogous to growth accounting, sometimes called development accounting, we can examine a group of countries at a given point in time and seek to explain what factors contribute to the differences in standard of living across countries. The economists Charles Jones and Dietz Vollrath conduct such an exercise using data for 2008 and come to the conclusion that while differences in investment rates and number of years of schooling can explain some of the cross-country differences in living standards, by far, the biggest factor is differences in TFP.[8] It is found that several countries have levels of TFP higher than the U.S., namely, Austria, Iceland, the Netherlands, Norway and Singapore.[9] Even in the presence of a technology gap, the level of TFP can be higher than that in a frontier economy if inputs in the technology follower are used very effectively. In developing a business-friendly environment and strong institutions, Singapore has been able to manage its resources efficiently (relative to the U.S.). Going forward, it is going to be having a mindset that seeks to learn best practices in the rest of the world and building upon them to create new and better-quality products that will enable Singapore to prosper.

---

[8]See Charles I. Jones and Dietz Vollrath, 2013, *Introduction to Economic Growth*, third edition, New York: W. W. Norton & Company.
[9]See Figure 3.2 of Jones and Vollrath (2013), p. 61.

Shifting Comparative Advantage

When Singapore began an industrialisation drive after becoming independent in 1965, a reliance on multinational firms to produce manufacturing products to sell into the world market was a key part of its economic strategy. The type of products the multinational firms produced, however, changed over the years, going from garments and textiles, to simple electronics, to disk drives, to semi-conductors and on to pharmaceutical products. It is this shift along the ladder of comparative advantage, along with the fact that Singapore is a price taker in the world market, that helps to explain why the return to capital could hold up for at least the first two to three decades of post-independence economic development despite rapid capital accumulation.[10]

In a one-good model of growth, such as the Solow growth model, the expansion of output of the same good driven by an increase in capital intensity runs into diminishing returns as we saw in the last section. However, when we recognise that there is a ladder of comparative advantage so that we can rank goods according to their relative capital intensity, a channel exists that generates structural change in the industrial structure as the economy's relative endowment of capital per worker increases. Suppose that the most labour-intensive good is clothing and the relatively capital-intensive good is simple electronics. With an economy that is relatively abundant in labour (compared to capital), such as Singapore in 1965, only clothing is produced. As capital was accumulated and the number of machines per worker increased, Singapore became competitive enough to produce both clothing and simple electronics. Instead of working in more factories producing clothing and facing diminishing returns, some workers moved into new factories producing simple electronics. Having more capital translated into an expansion of the relatively capital-intensive good (simple electronics) rather than more units of clothing thus avoiding diminishing returns. At some point, the economy's increase in relative capital abundance raised the real wage

---

[10]See Jaume Ventura, 1997, "Growth and Interdependence," *Quarterly Journal of Economics*, 112(1): 57–84.

sufficiently to make the production of labour-intensive clothing no longer profitable. However, the production of disk drives, which are relatively more capital-intensive compared to simple electronics, soon becomes economically viable. In this way, as the economy climbs up the ladder of comparative advantage, real wages rise and structural change occurs even as the return to capital holds up.

Could a relentless movement up the ladder of comparative advantage keep Singapore permanently on a path of sustained growth? There are two channels that might work to place a limit on such a view of economic growth. The first is that in any product line, such as disk drives, becoming a major supplier of the product itself drives down the world price of that export good. The worsening of the terms of trade, which is the natural outgrowth of quantity expansion itself, places a limit on growth as it signals diminishing returns. The second is that there is uncertainty about how high the ladder of comparative advantage is since the height of the ladder itself depends on future technological possibilities that are not forecastable. Nevertheless, staying alert to new technological developments and building the necessary human capital and physical infrastructure to become the base for producing the next product on the ladder will provide the impetus for future growth.

Human Capital

There are two different views about the contribution of human capital to economic growth. By human capital, we mean the level of skill an employee has in performing his job which is acquired both through formal schooling as well as on-the-job training. In the first view, human capital is analogous to physical capital. Just as an investment in physical capital augments the stock of physical capital used in production, spending an additional year of schooling is an investment activity that boosts the skill level of a worker. Empirical research suggests that an additional year of schooling raises a worker's wage by about 10 percent.[11] We can think of "effective labour" being

---

[11] See Jones and Vollrath, *op. cit.*, pp. 55–56.

given by the product of "raw labour" and the average skill level of a worker (determined by the worker's number of years of schooling). An increase in the average educational attainment of the Singapore workforce acts like an increase in the investment rate and can serve to generate transitional growth, on top of TFP growth, but cannot be counted on to produce sustained growth. In cross-country studies, it has been found that a difference in average years of schooling by eight years can explain why a country with the better educated workforce might be twice as rich as a country with the less educated workforce.[12]

The second view of the role played by human capital in explaining economic growth emphasises the stock of human capital and argues that a better-educated workforce has relative advantage in coping with novel situations.[13] Education, in this view, enables workers to learn new technologies that they might not have been exposed to before. Perhaps the industrial training as well as vocational training that accompanied the movement up the ladder of comparative advantage we discussed in the last section enabled the labour force to embrace changes even as one industry hollowed out to be replaced by another. Going forward, it is the ability to cope with novel situations that will position Singapore to enter a phase of growth that must be driven by innovative startups. As a bigger share of the labour force attains tertiary education, the process of learning from others enables each worker to do his work better. This knowledge spillover can serve to hold up the rate of productivity growth.

---

[12]See *ibid.*, p. 62. The classic paper applying the Solow model augmented to include human capital to study why some countries are rich and others are poor is N. Gregory Mankiw, David Romer and David N. Weil, 1992, "A Contribution to the Empirics of Economic Growth," *Quarterly Journal of Economics*, 107(2): 407–438.

[13]See Richard R. Nelson and Edmund S. Phelps, 1966, "Investment in Humans, Technological Diffusions, and Economic Growth," *American Economic Review*, 56(1/2): 69–75.

Small and Large Firms

While growth theory following the work of the economist Robert Solow has been aggregative in nature, the reality is that, in any industry, there is a size distribution of firms. The larger firms tend to be more productive and are net exporters while the smaller firms are less productive and sell only in the domestic market. The most productive firms, in fact, become multinational corporations and often produce in foreign affiliates to sell into the world market. In the early stages of Singapore's economic growth, the multinational firms based in Singapore brought along their technology blueprints when they set up factories to produce in Singapore to sell into the world market. Some local firms benefited when these multinational firms sub-contracted the production of some parts and components. Some local contract manufacturers could take advantage of economies of scale to produce certain standard parts and components to sell to different firms, both domestically as well as in overseas markets.

At the left tail of size distribution of firms, there exist many small firms that lack the ability to develop innovative products to gain new customers and apply good management practices to boost productivity in order to cover the cost of venturing into overseas markets. While many productive firms self-select into exporting, economists have found evidence that trade liberalisation itself helps firms to simultaneously break into overseas markets and increase resources devoted to research and development (R&D).[14] In this way, exporting and boosting productivity through R&D occur simultaneously. Going forward, a new source of growth will have to come from increasing the share of firms across different industries that cross the productivity threshold to be able to internationalise. Established firms may be hesitant to launch new and higher-quality products for fear that existing product lines might be displaced as customers shift away

---

[14]See Marc J. Melitz and Stephen J. Redding, "Heterogeneous Firms and Trade," in *Handbook of International Economics*, Volume 4, Gita Gopinath, Elhanan Helpman, and Kenneth Rogoff (eds.), Amsterdam: Elsevier, pp. 1–54.

their purchases. Small firms and new startups have greater incentive to find new niches. However, they are limited by the availability of financing. An industry consortium might be able to pool resources to provide training that will help individual firms to lower cost. By boosting each firm's productivity, more firms will be able to cover the fixed cost to sell into overseas markets.

Chapter 4

Jobs and Business Fluctuations

Holding a job is a central part of a fulfilling life. Yet, a nation's ability to deliver a steady stream of good jobs is not a given. At independence, Singapore's unemployment rate was close to 10 percent. It steadily declined to about three percent by the mid-1980s. Against this backdrop, the unemployment rate in Western Europe hovered around two to three percent in the 1950s and 1960s. Nevertheless, from the early 1970s, the unemployment rate gradually crawled upwards to reach double-digit levels by the mid-1980s. We would like to understand what forces brought down Singapore's unemployment rate, without igniting inflationary pressures, and the future prospects for jobs.

In 1985, the unemployment rate spiked upwards when Singapore entered a sharp recession. Subsequently, there were other recessionary shocks that caused a rise in layoffs — in 1998, 2003 and 2009 — and a rise in the unemployment rate although not to levels as high as in 1985. We would like to understand the nature of shocks that can produce economic recessions and the propagation mechanisms through which the economic shocks work to slow down the economy. The chapter then discusses the policy measures to tackle these recessions.

Natural Rate of Unemployment

How is a country's natural rate of unemployment determined? The theory used to guide our thinking about the determination of the natural rate of unemployment builds around the notion that in any modern economy, there are firms looking for suitable workers to fill newly-created job vacancies or vacancies left open because of quits and workers who are looking for suitable jobs. However, the matching of workers to job vacancies takes time. A convenient construct called an aggregate matching function relates the number of new hires each period to the number of unemployed workers and the number of job vacancies. Empirical evidence suggests that the matching function is constant returns to scale, that is, a doubling of the number of job vacancies and the number of unemployed workers doubles the number of successful job matches.[1] The probability at any given point in time that a job vacancy can be filled is then given by the number of matches per job vacancy, which is, in turn, inversely related to the number of job vacancies per unemployed worker. The latter is conveniently described as a measure of labour market tightness. When the labour market is tight, firms find it more difficult to fill a job vacancy.

Suppose that a firm creates a new job vacancy. It has to pay an upfront cost to advertise for the position and devote time to interview potential job candidates. The expected benefit to the firm of filling the job with a suitable job candidate is the surplus from the filled job multiplied by the probability that a job vacancy is filled. The surplus, in turn, is given by the excess of the present discounted value of the revenue generated by the newly-employed worker over the present discounted value of the wage bill incurred by hiring that worker. The discount rate applied to derive the present value of the future revenue and wage is the sum of the real interest rate and the job separation rate. Free entry ensures that the expected present discounted value of the surplus, adjusted for the probability of filling the job vacancy, is equal to the upfront cost of advertising for and assessing the suitability of potential job candidates.

---

[1]See Barbara Petrongolo and Christopher A. Pissarides, 2001, "Looking into the Black Box: A Survey of the Matching Function," *Journal of Economic Literature*, 39(2): 390–431.

From the early phase of Singapore's economic development, it might be argued that Singapore's catch-up growth caught most participants by surprise so that the present discounted value of revenue generated from filled positions grew relative to the present discounted value of wages. Given the real interest rate and job separation rate, this meant that the measure of labour market tightness — the number of job vacancies per unemployed worker — increased. The vacancy rate, defined as the number of job vacancies per member of the workforce, is negatively related to the unemployment rate, defined as the number of unemployed workers per member of the workforce via the Beveridge curve. Consequently, as labour market tightness increases, the vacancy rate increases and the unemployment rate decreases.

Future challenges will come from a more rapid pace of creative destruction. In the search-matching framework, this means that the discount rate used to discount future surpluses from successful job matches will increase as job turnover becomes more rapid. Holding everything else constant, this would lead to a less tight labour market and, consequently, a higher rate of unemployment. Avoiding this outcome will require that firms' productivity levels rise somewhat faster than pay increases. This means that Singapore needs to continue its efforts to restructure the economy so that many small firms can develop innovative products, apply good management practices, and venture into overseas markets to boost revenues. Wage aspirations also have to keep in step with a slower pace of growth with the end of the catch-up phase of growth. Workers need to be willing to be retrained to acquire new skills to take up newly-created job vacancies.

Better job matching also enables the economy to achieve simultaneously a lower job vacancy rate and lower unemployment rate. Unlike a big country like the U.S. where taking a new job might mean leaving New York to work in California, being a city state means that the matching of workers to job vacancies is less costly in Singapore. In an environment where job destruction occurs more frequently, it is necessary to create a system that seeks to minimise the typical duration of unemployment. Prolonged unemployment leads to skill obsolescence and has non-pecuniary costs like discouragement and disengagement from the workplace. Since there are social costs to long-term unemployment, there is an economic case for the government to give employment and training subsidies to firms to hire retrenched workers. By giving financial incentives, the government can build up a pool of firms that are ready to hire and train workers who are matched to them.

Shocks and Propagation Mechanisms

The growth process itself is uneven so that even when the economy is not in a recession we observe job turnover arising not only from workers who quit their jobs to look for another but also from businesses that fail. In an efficient economy, if the revenue generated from the cooperation between labour and capital falls below the opportunity costs that these resources can earn elsewhere in the economy, the firm should shut down to free the labour and capital to be employed in an alternative business venture. However, there is often relationship specificity or technological specificity so that when a firm shuts down, the resources freed up cannot earn its ex-ante opportunity costs. In such an environment, there tends to be excessive job destruction during economic downturns.

In the short run, there is evidence of nominal wage and price stickiness.[2] In the presence of nominal wage and price rigidity, "effective demand" plays a vital role in affecting an economy's output. In an open economy like Singapore, components of aggregate demand, which make up effective demand, include consumption, investment, government spending and net exports. Investment can be classified as private and public investment, on one hand, and domestic and foreign direct investment on the other hand. A decline in each of the components of aggregate demand causes the economy's total real GDP to fall.

---

[2]See Peter Klenow and Benjamin Malin, 2011, "Microeconomic Evidence on Price-Setting," in *Handbook of Monetary Economics*, Volume 3A, Benjamin Friedman and Michael Woodford (eds.), Amsterdam: Elsevier, pp. 231–284.

Suppose that there is a recession in Singapore's major trading partners. As a result, there is a fall in net exports. Then what happens? Let us focus on a case of nominal wage rigidity. With firms based in Singapore finding that their output is in excess supply, there is a downward pressure on the prices that they set. In turn, with nominal wages being rigid, it is no longer profitable to hire the same number of workers as before. Layoffs increase. This is a demand-induced recession.

There are also supply-induced recessions. One familiar example comes from a sharp increase in oil prices. Oil is an intermediate good used in the production of final goods and services. When its price increases, the bigger energy bill eats into the firm's profitability. To cover this additional cost, the firm increases its price markup over the unit labour cost. However, a higher price-labour cost markup can only be achieved at a lower real wage paid to workers. Given a positively-sloped wage-setting curve, this implies a rise in unemployment.

In the review of the causes of Singapore's 1985 recession, one factor pointed to was an increase in wages that outstripped productivity growth.[3] Given marginal physical productivity of labour, a rise in nominal wages must be accompanied by a rise in the relative price of the product if the firm is to remain profitable. In the absence of relative price increases, and lacking any productivity improvement, a rise in nominal wages would lead to layoff of workers. With fewer workers getting to work with the stock of machines, there would be a compensating improvement in labour productivity to justify the higher pay of employed workers. Going forward, supporting wage increases by higher productivity performance remains necessary if we are to avoid a supply-induced recession.

Fighting Recessions

The policy Singapore adopted in response to a significant decline in aggregate demand, namely, by implementing a national programme

---

[3]See Report of the Economic Committee, 1986, *The Singapore Economy: New Directions*, Singapore Ministry of Trade and Industry.

of lowering wage costs, is somewhat uncommon both among emerging and developed economies. Suppose an economy is hit by a recessionary shock that leads to a fall in aggregate demand. Economies that follow a conventional Taylor Rule would progressively lower the short-term nominal interest rate to spur aggregate demand both by effectively lowering the real interest rate and by weakening domestic currencies as international capital flows out (under a flexible exchange rate regime). Conventional fiscal policy takes the form of boosting aggregate demand either, directly, by increasing government purchases or, indirectly, by a cut in income taxes. It is not often the case that a programme to directly reduce wage costs would be a centrepiece of a national economic recovery effort.

How does the use of wage subsidies — the term for lowering wage costs through policy intervention — fit into the corpus of macroeconomic theory? In particular, since the seminal work on micro-foundations for macroeconomics, summarised in the Phelps (1970) volume, the Phillips curve relationship or aggregate supply curve is derived from optimising decisions of all economic agents — both producers and employees.[4] How does the introduction of a wage subsidy scheme during a recession affect the personnel decision of firms with regards to hiring and the decision of employees with regards to quitting? How does the producer adjust its mark-up in response to the implementation of a wage subsidy scheme?

There are two main features that characterise the model economy we would like to use to analyse the theoretical effects of introducing a wage subsidy scheme to fight recessions: dispersed information and the absence of a Walrasian auctioneer.[5] Without a fictitious Walrasian auctioneer to call out prices to clear markets instantaneously, each firm must adopt a wage policy (to combat quitting)

---

[4]See Edmund S. Phelps, et al., 1970, *Microeconomic Foundations of Employment and Inflation Theory*, New York: W. W. Norton.

[5]My discussion of the use of wage subsidies as a counter-recessionary tool draws on Hian Teck Hoon, 2014, "Wage Subsidies as a Tool to Fight Recessions," in *Macroeconomic Review*, Volume XIII, Issue 2: 91–96 published by the Economic Policy Group, Monetary Authority of Singapore.

and a product pricing policy. The result is that job rationing — hence involuntary unemployment — emerges and price-marginal cost mark-ups vary as firms exercise their market power. As information is dispersed, no single economic actor initially knows what the others in the economy know. Yet, in setting wages and product prices, each firm does not want to be caught paying its employees too little (for fear of precipitating labour turnover) or charging its customers too much (for fear of losing market share). The consequence of the dispersed information, also called incomplete information, is that each firm often gets its expectations of wages and prices prevailing elsewhere in the economy wrong — a state of expectational disequilibrium. So long as the economy is in such a state, the actual unemployment rate will deviate from the natural rate of unemployment.

There is a certain rhythm in the model economy with regards to when wages are set and pricing decisions are made. Wages are typically set for a year before any new pay adjustment occurs. Product prices may be adjusted more often than once a year but typically not on a daily basis. Moreover, the date for wage and price setting occurs throughout the year in a non-synchronous manner. The result of the staggering in wage and price setting throughout the year is that, even when information flow has become reasonably complete, the economy exhibits some form of nominal wage and price stickiness. In response, say, to a negative aggregate demand shock, average wages and prices do not immediately fall by enough to restore the economy to its potential output level. Wage and price staggering, therefore, imparts to the economy persistence in the output gap, that is, a recession can become long-drawn in the absence of any policy intervention. In this context, Singapore has been willing to take decisive steps to intervene in the economy to hasten recovery by providing wage subsidies.

An increase in the wage subsidy acts to shift right the aggregate supply schedule. This is because a wage subsidy drives a wedge between the real demand wage and the real supply wage, on the one hand, and it also gives firms the incentive to reduce mark-ups, on the other hand. We can call this channel through which the wage subsidy operates a boosting of labour demand channel. Two other channels through which a wage subsidy scheme to fight recessions might minimise unemployment and boost employment are: (a) Cash-flow channel; and (b) Signalling channel. If there are firms that are credit constrained, but are otherwise healthy, the provision of wage subsidies enables them to avoid going into the red during the recession. Hence, layoffs are avoided. By implementing a national wage subsidy scheme, policy-makers, who have the resources to collect data enabling them to discern that a shock is not industry or sector specific but is economy-wide in its impact, can convey information to firms that helps to narrow the expectational disequilibrium.

To be able to finance wage subsidies to fight recessions, the government needs to generate fiscal surpluses in good times when tax revenues are growing (at given tax rates). When hit by a recessionary shock, the government will then have the fiscal resources to act decisively to bring about a quick economic recovery. In normal times, economic restructuring can be part and parcel of the regular rhythm of reallocating resources to their most productive uses.

Chapter 5

Wage Growth and Wage Inequality

A feature of Singapore's growth experience is that the wage share has been relatively constant. Given this, the steady increase in the real GDP per worker since independence has been accompanied by real wage growth. In the absence of technological progress and the opportunity for international trade, a steady increase in the capital-labour ratio leads to real wage growth. Nevertheless, as capital accumulation faces diminishing returns, the real wage growth peters out in the absence of technological progress and trading opportunities. However, Singapore has, indeed, been vitally integrated into the global economy in its economic development. As a result, the economy has moved up the ladder of comparative advantage even as the capital-labour ratio increased both as a result of domestic investment as well as foreign direct investment. In addition, as Singapore moved towards the technological frontier, the closing of the technology gap has also meant that, at given capital-labour ratio, the real wage has been pulled up.

While the fruits of economic progress have been broadly shared by the broad swathe of workers, the gains have differed across workers with different skill levels. Up to the turn of the twenty-first century, wage gains have been stronger for less-skilled workers compared to higher-skilled workers. Thus, the wage gap, as measured both by the wage ratio between high-skill and low-skill workers as well as the wage ratio between middle-skill and low-skill workers, steadily decreased until around 2000. From that point on, the wage gap began to increase. A shift in comparative advantage resulting from human capital accumulation and skill-biased technological progress might be contributing factors to the reversal of the narrowing wage gap.

Another feature of workers' remuneration that has been observed in many countries is that apparently similar workers obtain different wage earnings if they work in different industries. Secretaries, for example, working in a capital-intensive industry are paid more than their counterparts elsewhere in the economy.[1] Moreover, the heterogeneous pay of similar workers is observed across firms even in the same industry with workers having the same educational qualification being paid more if they are employed in larger firms that sell into overseas markets.[2]

Comparative Advantage

Since trade in goods and services is so important in Singapore's economic development, a discussion of wage growth and wage inequality requires a return to the concept of comparative advantage introduced earlier in Chapter 3. If Singapore were producing only a single product, say textiles, using capital and labour and selling all of its output domestically, then GDP per worker would rise but at a diminishing rate. At independence, Singapore attracted textile and garment manufacturers from Hong Kong and Taiwan to open factories to work with its workers. With a steady flow of investment equipping a growing workforce with machinery to work with, the marginal productivity of workers increased. The first factory to open up reaped high returns to capital, which encouraged further investment. The buildup of the physical capital stock per worker raised workers' remuneration. If the output was all sold domestically, the subsequent factories would face lower returns as diminishing marginal productivity of capital sets in. Thus, workers' remuneration would reach a plateau.

---

[1] See Alan B. Krueger and Lawrence H. Summers, 1988, "Efficiency Wages and the Inter-Industry Wage Structure," *Econometrica*, 56(2): 259–293.

[2] See Dale T. Mortensen, 2003, *Wage Dispersion: Why Are Similar Workers Paid Differently?*, Cambridge, MA: MIT Press.

In fact, Singapore's textiles and garments were sold into the global market. Its exports of textiles and garments were exchanged internationally for relatively more capital-intensive imports such as televisions. Textiles and garments are relatively more labour-intensive compared to televisions in the sense that at a given wage-rental ratio, the production of a television uses more capital per worker than the production of a unit of garment. Compared to advanced economies like the U.S. and the U.K. in the 1960s, which were relatively well endowed in physical capital, Singapore was relatively more abundant in labour. As a result, in the absence of trade, textiles produced in Singapore would be relatively cheap. In contrast, with relatively scarce capital, a television produced domestically would be relatively expensive. Under international trade, Singapore would be the net exporter of textiles and garments. This trade pattern is consistent with the theory of comparative advantage. International trade in products, in effect, serves as an indirect means of trading the services of capital and labour. With Singapore being relatively abundant in labour in the 1960s, trade in goods enabled Singapore to export indirectly labour services in exchange for capital services. From the perspective of understanding the effects of trade based on comparative advantage, the important point is that being able to sell textiles and garments in the world market lifts up the real wage of workers because it fetches a better relative price than if all textiles were sold domestically.

If Singapore were selling only textiles and garments into the world market, an improvement in its terms of trade, that is, an increase in the world relative price of textiles and garments in terms of televisions, would further lift up real wages. However, the world market determines the relative price of textiles and garments in terms of televisions based on global demand and supply conditions. If there is a glut in the world market for textiles and garments, Singapore would experience a decline in real wages.

At given world prices, the increase in capital stock relative to the supply of labour means that the share of labour employed in textile manufacturing would decline as more workers get to be employed in producing televisions, the relatively capital-intensive good. At some stage, the greater abundance of capital relative to labour supply makes the production of textiles uncompetitive. It now becomes viable to produce televisions and another product that is relatively capital-intensive even when compared to televisions, say, disk drives. Singapore now indirectly exports the services of both human and physical capital in exchange for imports of the services of unskilled labour from foreign labour-abundant countries. As this happens, the economy's real wage increases relative to the real wage earned when the economy's relative factor endowment made only textiles and televisions viable. One can now imagine a whole ladder of comparative advantage starting with textiles and garments at the bottom rung, television in the next rung, then disk drives, and so on. The increase in the abundance of capital relative to labour supply moves the economy up the ladder of comparative advantage and, along with this, the real wage steadily increases. A remarkable feature of this continuous process of industrial restructuring means that there is a mechanism that allows the economy to avoid diminishing marginal productivity of capital as the economy moves away from producing goods at lower rungs of the ladder of comparative advantage to new products at given world prices.[3] Real wages also rise as the economy moves up along the ladder of comparative advantage.

While industries can be ranked on the basis of their relative capital intensity, there is another way of ranking industries that can throw light on the wage gap between higher-skilled and less-skilled workers. We can call the wage gap a skills premium or a wage premium. We can rank industries on the basis of skills intensity. At a given wage premium, some industries employ relatively more skilled workers compared to less-skilled workers. With Singapore's labour force having relatively fewer average number of years of schooling in the early phase of its industrialisation, its comparative advantage was in relatively less-skilled-labour-intensive products. Being able to export such products meant that the wage premium was smaller

---

[3]See Jaume Ventura, 1997, "Growth and Interdependence," *Quarterly Journal of Economics*, 112(1): 57–84.

under international trade than under autarky. However, taking world relative prices as given, there would have to be a steady improvement in Singapore's terms of trade to explain the declining wage premium until 2000 when the wage premium began to increase. Based on the notion of the ladder of comparative advantage where lower rungs represent goods that are relatively less-skilled-labour-intensive, the steady improvement in the educational attainment of Singapore's workers should mean a steady rise of the wage premium.

How then to explain why the reversal in the downward trend of the wage premium occurred around 2000? Recall that there has been a steady increase in physical capital that took place at a faster pace than the increase in average number of years of schooling. It is possible that the machinery installed in factories in the first few decades were complementary to less-skilled labour since the economy was relatively abundant in less-skilled labour in the first few decades of economic development. The complementarity between physical capital and less-skilled labour means that the rapid investment in physical capital led to a rise in the relative demand for unskilled labour that offset the effect on wage premium arising from the movement up the ladder of comparative advantage. By 2000, the workforce had become relatively better educated and this channel came to a halt. Subsequent capital investments were complementary to skilled labour as Singapore's pool of skilled labour grew, as reflected in the increase in the average number of years of schooling and a sharp increase of the workforce having tertiary education after 1990. Going forward, capital investments are likely to complement skilled labour and thus the wage gap between high-skill and low-skill workers will increase. Whereas market forces and technology in the first three-and-a-half decades acted to narrow the wage gap, they are now likely to widen wage inequality. This means that policy interventions in the form of wage income supplements as well as employment and training subsidies will be required to boost the take-home pay of low-wage workers. As market forces act to shift wage gains disproportionately towards high-skill workers, there is a case for an increase in top marginal tax rates to finance social interventions to foster economic inclusion.

Technology

We saw in Chapter 3 that Singapore's economic growth could be represented as a catch-up towards the technology frontier, in the process closing the technology gap. The growth of neutral technology, that is, technology that boosts both the marginal productivity of labour as well as the marginal productivity of capital about equally, offers another channel to escape the diminishing returns to capital in our thought experiment.[4] At constant technology, if Singapore increased its capital-labour ratio and produced textiles to sell into the domestic market, real wages would rise but reach a plateau as diminishing returns to capital set in and the economy reaches a steady-state level of capital intensity. However, if technology is steadily improving in a neutral fashion, then the marginal productivity of capital is boosted thus further encouraging an increase in the capital-labour ratio. Consequently, the real wage can steadily improve both on account of capital deepening as well as on account of the neutral improvement in technology.

In practice, the improvement in technology helped anchor the textile industry in Singapore for a longer time period by boosting international competitiveness than if technology were constant. Yet, the growing relative abundance of physical capital most likely meant that industrial restructuring ultimately led to newer industries on the upper rungs of the ladder of comparative advantage replacing those on the lower rungs.

The widening of the wage gap has been observed in the advanced economies since the 1980s. There is some consensus that the cause is the onslaught of skill-biased technological progress. Given a relative supply of higher-skilled to less-skilled workers, an upward shift of the relative demand for higher-skilled to less-skilled labour would lead to an increase of the wage premium. Consider the entry of the computer age with the wide adoption of computers in the workplace. Skilled labour would be in high demand. As a result, skill-biased technological progress would lead to a widening wage gap. Such a

---

[4]This is referred to as Hicks-neutral technical progress.

channel could have also played a part in the increase in the wage premium observed in Singapore since 2000.[5] Going forward, the arrival of robotics and advances in artificial intelligence will play an important role in shaping wages. At one level, the introduction of robots that add to human labour drives down wages as robots substitute for workers in production. On the other hand, there are multiplicative robots that act to augment labour power in performing certain tasks. By raising workers' productivity, such robots increase the marginal contribution of human labour and boost their pay rates.

Residual Wage Inequality

How do we explain why similar workers are paid differently? One explanation appeals to the fact that there is imperfect information in the search and matching process between firms looking for suitable employees and workers looking for their ideal jobs. Suppose that workers who are currently employed are able also to search for a job and can make job-to-job transitions. In such a setting, a firm that makes a higher wage offer to similar workers would be more likely to have the job offer accepted. As a consequence, we would observe that larger firms pay their workers more.[6] A related explanation is that, while workers have identical educational qualifications, they have different characteristics that make some of them more likely to be successful employees in their contributions to the firm's profitability. Larger firms may have better resources to invest in screening the potential job candidates and, therefore, find a better match to fill their job vacancies.

Yet another explanation that has been offered to explain why there exist interindustry wage differentials falls under the category of efficiency wage theories. Consider a firm that hires a new worker but

---

[5] See an analysis of the role of skill-biased technological progress in explaining the rise in wage premium in the advanced economies in Daron Acemoglu and David Autor, 2011, "Skills, Tasks and Technologies: Implications for Employment and Earnings," in *Handbook of Labor Economics*, Volume 4B, Orley Ashenfelter and David Card (eds.), Amsterdam: Elsevier, pp. 1043–1171.

[6] See Dale T. Mortensen, *op cit.*

has to make a firm-specific investment in training the worker before he can become a productive employee at the firm. However, there is a risk that after the firm has incurred the firm-specific investment to train the worker, he quits the firm and leaves for an alternative job opportunity elsewhere because of shifting job preferences. In order to induce its employees to stay at the firm after being trained, the firm offers an incentive wage calculated to balance the expected contribution of the worker to the cost of firm-specific training. One consequence of such a wage policy is to drive the prevailing wage above the market-clearing wage with the result that there is job rationing. Some workers become involuntarily unemployed. Across firms, the nature and costliness of offering firm-specific training might differ so the wage calculated to minimise labour turnover would be different across firms. As a result, similar workers are paid differently depending on which industry they are employed in.

Behind the strategy to help small and medium-sized firms internationalise is the aim to enable them to operate at a larger scale. By selling into a larger market, the firm can reduce average cost and increase profitability. Higher profitability leads to entry of new firms that compete for workers thus driving up wage earnings. As firms expand, they invest resources to develop new and better products. Their human resource departments invest in screening workers to find the best fit for the new job tasks. Workers of the future might have to move often between jobs. While some new employers the workers seek out are in industries that place a premium on their past work experience, there are other potential employers in entirely new businesses that do not value their past work experience. This has implications for the wage profile over time of future workers, where wage earnings do not necessarily increase with work experience. Workers will have to take into account greater variability of pay rates over their working life when making consumption-saving decisions.

Part II

Finding Political Consensus to Embrace Economic Openness

Chapter 6

Economic Openness

What caused Singapore's catch up to the world technology frontier after its independence? Arguably, the policy to welcome multinational corporations to set up factories in Singapore to produce for the world market is one key factor behind its catch up. What the economic openness enabled Singapore to do was to facilitate technology transfer or the international flow of ideas. As an economy that has caught up to the world technology frontier, Singapore is now in a phase where it has to begin to generate indigenous innovation. The notion that ideas for creating new and better products and processes comes from people means that Singapore would need to be a place that would attract innovative individuals to develop startups here. If it is the case that ideas diffuse across society from interactions among individuals, then the exposure to innovative people helps Singapore become an economy that routinely creates a flow of new ideas.

Small and medium-sized enterprises play a central role in the innovative process. The presence of Marshallian externalities means that investments at the industry level have positive spillovers that benefit all the firms in the economy. The size of the domestic market limits the extent to which average costs of each small and medium-sized enterprise can be reduced. By selling into the world market, the industry is able to enjoy economies of scale that translate into further reduction of firms' average costs. Selling into the world market also means greater competition for small and medium-sized enterprises. This competition will drive some firms that are unproductive to exit from the industry. The more productive firms will become more profitable as they gain market share. Thus, self selection under international competition also raises the average productivity of Singapore's industries.

In the next stage of growth, multinational corporations continue to play a vital role in the Singapore economy as they supply good jobs with good pay. At the same time, as some of the small and medium-sized enterprises become successful in exporting and expand their scale, it might become more profitable for them to set up multinational firms abroad rather than export into these markets. The fixed cost of setting up a multinational firm abroad might be less than the total variable trade costs of exporting. The outward flow of foreign direct investment might occur to take advantage of lower costs of production of certain stages of the production value chain, as well as to use proprietary knowledge developed by a Singaporean firm.

Flow of Ideas

Ideas are fundamentally different from conventional goods because they are nonrivalrous and only partially excludable. This notion of rivalry and excludability differentiating conventional goods from ideas lies at the heart of the economist Paul Romer's work on endogenous growth.[1] A major result from the neoclassical growth models (associated with the work of Robert Solow) is that the rate of growth of per capita income is determined by the rate of technological growth. To endogenise the rate of technological growth, we need to face two challenges. The first challenge is to see that one way of interpreting "technology" is to say that the level of technology is tantamount to the "stock of ideas" — ideas about the kinds of products that can be produced, for example. Ideas, however, are *nonrivalrous* in the sense that if I possess an idea, you too can possess the same idea I have (by copying my idea) without my having less

---

[1]See Paul M. Romer, 1990, "Endogenous Technological Change," *Journal of Political Economy*, 98(5), Part 2: S71–S102.

of it. This makes an idea different from a conventional good, in that a conventional good is rivalrous. For example, an apple is a rivalrous good. If I have an apple, you can have this same apple only if I give mine away to you. Because ideas are non-rivalrous, this means that if one worker has a new idea, he can, in principle, share that new idea with one hundred other workers without losing his new idea in any way. The first challenge we are confronted with in endogenizing the rate of technological growth is that with increasing returns to scale, perfect competition breaks down. One of the most important contributions by Paul Romer is to show how firms have an incentive to create new ideas under *imperfect* competition with some form of patent protection. In the next phase of Singapore's growth, both public investment in R&D well as firms' R&D activities will take on greater significance in generating productivity improvements.

The second challenge is to show that patent protection only gives firms with the patent protection *partial excludability* from their ideas. This is because later innovators can "stand on the shoulders of giants" when they develop new ideas or blueprints without the need to "reinvent the wheel". Even though firms with patents can legally prevent other firms from directly copying their ideas, there is some "leakage" of ideas into a common pool that later innovators can take advantage of when they try to develop further new ideas. The bulk of R&D is performed by the G7 countries — the United States, Canada, France, Germany, Italy, the United Kingdom and Japan. Following the argument of Romer, a very important benefit of economic openness is the adoption of ideas developed abroad. One way Singapore benefits is for later generations of innovators to build on the pool of ideas that are already developed elsewhere.[2] Singapore sets up centres overseas so that its students can spend a portion of time there to learn about new markets and be exposed to innovative projects there, and can return home to see how they can build upon these ideas to develop new products and processes. There are also ideas about how to organise various aspects of society that Singapore

---

[2]Paul M. Romer, 2010, "What Parts of Globalization Matter for Catch-Up Growth?" *American Economic Review: Papers and Proceedings*, 100(2): 94–98.

can draw upon such as how innovative societies like the U.S. bring together financiers and people with fresh ideas to launch innovative businesses.

Flow of Goods and Services

There are important gains from trade based on comparative advantage. In turn, comparative advantage can arise from technological differences across countries as well as from differences in relative factor endowments. In the early decades of Singapore's economic development, it had comparative advantage in relatively less-skilled-labour-intensive goods. The ability to sell garments and textiles into the world market in exchange for more sophisticated electronic and electrical goods enabled Singapore workers to achieve a higher real consumption wage — the wage in terms of the typical basket of goods consumed. With an increase in educational attainment, Singapore's comparative advantage has shifted towards relatively skill-intensive goods. It is now the ability to export precision engineering products in exchange for garments from abroad that raises consumers' welfare.

While international trade generates overall gains for the economy as a whole, certain factors of production can be hurt by international trade. Consider two types of workers with specific skills: Type-H skills and Type-L skills. Workers with Type-H skills produce good X with a fixed labour coefficient while workers with Type-L skills produce good Y with yet another fixed labour coefficient. In the absence of trade, with a situation of autarky, there is a domestically determined relative price of good X in terms of good Y. Let's say that, under international trade, the economy is a net-exporter of good X. The result is that the real wage of the Type-H worker remains unchanged when measured in terms of good X (given the fixed labour coefficient) but increases when measured in terms of good Y. Hence, the real consumption wage of the Type-H worker increases as a result of international trade. As for the Type-L worker, his real wage remains unchanged when measured in terms of good Y, the good that he is employed to produce, and decreases when measured in terms of good X. Hence, the real consumption wage of the Type-L worker is reduced as a result of international trade. Moreover, when the relative price of good X in terms of good Y increases, that is, when there is an improvement in the terms of trade, the real consumption wage of Type-H workers rises but the real consumption wage of type-L workers is further reduced. In such an economy, providing training for Type-L workers to acquire the skills of Type-H workers will enable them to be employed in producing good X and thus enjoy gains from trade. To foster political support for economic openness, government subsidies for retraining of workers to acquire new skills will be a vital part of Singapore's next phase of economic development.

Because of the heterogeneity of the firms within any given industry with a whole distribution of productivity levels, there are firms that are competitive enough only to sell within the domestic market. There is a cutoff productivity level above which more productive firms are able both to sell domestically as well as in the overseas market. A reduction in trade costs has the effect of raising the cutoff productivity level; moreover, the least productive firms exit the market. The firms that survive the stiffer competition of trade liberalisation enjoy higher profits. They pay their workers more. There are also gains in productivity resulting from learning by exporting. Both these channels imply that greater economic openness raises the average productivity level of industries in Singapore.

Flow of Capital

Singapore has been a beneficiary of the inflow of foreign direct investments over the past decades. The multinational corporations brought along standard technology in the early days and then gradually more sophisticated technology as the depth of skills of the Singaporean workforce grew. In addition, they also offered middle-level management jobs. As the multinational firms based in Singapore are large and more productive, they also paid similar workers more. This suggests that even as a major boost to Singapore's overall productivity improvement will come from helping firms at the low end of the productivity distribution expand their scale by selling into overseas markets, attracting foreign direct investment continues to be very important for delivering jobs with high pay. Moreover workers gain experience from working in multinational corporations and can carry over their understanding of good management practices and implement them when they make career moves to join startups.

As small and medium-sized enterprises succeed in exporting into the world market, their scale will increase. Since there are trade costs incurred in exporting, some of the successful firms might find that it is more profitable to actually set up a multinational firm in the overseas market. In part, this would be to take advantage of lower costs of producing certain less-skilled components in the production value chain in neighbouring economies with a relative abundance of less to semi-skilled labour. As the rate of innovation increases domestically, there might be proprietary knowledge that is developed so that Singaporean firms find it optimal to set up multinational firms to produce these components rather than buy from unaffiliated foreign firms. Some firms might start by exporting into regional markets. As they come to understand these markets better and learn to tailor products to suit their regional customers, they might take advantage of lower costs in these markets to produce and sell there directly.

The development of the financial sector means that Singapore will continue to be open to the international flow of financial capital (on top of inflow of foreign direct investment). The free international mobility of capital means that by choosing to manage the exchange rate as a tool to achieve low and stable inflation, the Monetary Authority of Singapore cannot keep its domestic interest rate different from the world interest rate. While giving up direct control of the domestic interest rate, Singapore has to rely on fiscal policy such as bringing forward public investment projects during recessionary shocks and wage subsidies such as the Jobs Credit to fight recessions. However, the further development of the financial sector will be important for financing of business projects as Singapore develops indigenous innovation. A vibrant financial sector also creates good jobs for workers.

Flow of People

The notion that it is people who produce ideas is beautifully expressed by the economist Edmund Phelps in a 1968 article about population increase:[3]

> One can hardly imagine, I think, how poor we would be today were it not for the rapid population growth of the past to which we owe the enormous number of technological advances enjoyed today. Certainly until the present time we have been living, and possibly will live for some time into the future, in circumstances of increasing returns to scale by virtue of these technological considerations. ... If I could re-do the history of the world, halving population size each year from the beginning of time on some random basis, I would not do it for fear of losing Mozart in the process. No improvement of our dirty air and our traffic congestion could compensate me for that!

The importance of a large population to support the creation of ideas, which in turn propels productivity growth, can best be grasped by asking what caused the rise in living standards beginning from the First Industrial Revolution in Britain and spread to other parts of the world. The economic model introduced by the British scholar Thomas Malthus can be used to organise our thinking.[4] The Malthusian model assumes that population growth is increasing with income per capita above a subsistence level. The production of goods requires land and labour. It has the property that output per capita is inversely related to population size given the fixed stock of land. We see that the steady-state population is proportional to the amount of land. Larger land areas would be capable of supporting larger populations. In addition, if technology improves, this increases the size of steady-state population as well. Better technology means that the economy can support more people on the same area of land because it makes that land more productive. Note that, in steady

---

[3]Edmund S. Phelps, 1968, "Population Increase," *Canadian Journal of Economics* 1(3): 497–518.

[4]See Thomas Malthus, 1798, *An Essay on the Principle of Population*, London: J. Johnson.

state, income per capita is equal to the subsistence level. It does not respond to either the amount of land or level of technology.

Why is it that living standards in the Malthusian economy remain stagnant at the subsistence level and are not affected by having more land or better technology? This is the result of having population growth positively related to income per capita. If income per capita were greater than the subsistence level, then population would grow as people would have relatively larger families. Given a fixed stock of land, and given technology, the larger population leads to declining income per capita as the marginal product of labour declines. Starting at an initial steady state, better technology means that income per capita initially rises above subsistence level thus leading to population growth. As the population grows, income per capita declines, and population growth declines as well. Eventually, the economy reaches a new steady-state level with a larger population size and steady-state income per capita returns to subsistence level. Technology improvement in the Malthusian model leads to only temporary gains in living standards, but permanent gains in population size. This is what we observe historically in the Malthusian era, as living standards were stagnant for long stretches of time but the absolute population size continued to increase.

Now, let the growth rate of technology depend positively on the size of the population so the assumption is in the tradition of "ideas are found in people". The more people there are, the faster the rate at which new ideas are discovered. We can then show that the growth rate of the population is positively related to the size of the population.[5] To take account of the fact that after 1970, the positive relationship between population growth rate and the size of population does not hold, Jones and Vollrath incorporate more realistic population growth rates such that at low levels of living standards, population growth increases with income per capita but at high levels of living standards, population growth decreases

---

[5]See Jones and Vollrath, *op cit.*, which updates a chart (originally from Michael Kremer), Figure 8.5, which shows that this positive relationship holds in the historical data until around 1970 when the relationship breaks down.

with income per capita. With the more realistic population growth rates, Jones and Vollrath show how an economy can transit from Malthusian stagnation to sustained growth. In the beginning, the population is very small and technological growth is very slow. At some stage, as population size increases, the rate of technological growth increases until the world reaches a situation where it is larger than the maximum rate of population growth. A demographic transition leading towards lower population growth sets in as income per capita continues to increase and the population growth settles down to the rate of world population growth.

If we accept the historical record as being supportive of the hypothesis that it is people who generate ideas, then the projected decline in Singapore's population on account of below replacement total fertility rate implies fewer innovators in future. This concern can in part be addressed by creating an environment where more people work on creating ideas so that the innovation intensity — the number of new ideas per person — increases. However, as the flow of new ideas per unit time must grow to keep up with a growing stock of ideas to maintain a given rate of growth, we would need to also expand the number of innovators. This requires a two-prong approach of boosting total fertility as well as managing a controlled flow immigrants. Singapore would benefit from facilitating the process of ideas creation by welcoming innovators from abroad.

Chapter 7

Coping with Opportunism

In an economy characterised by creative destruction, jobs are destroyed even as new jobs are created. A feature of the U.S. economy is that hiring and job separations are positively correlated both across firms and over time.[1] This is consistent with an economy characterised by churn. Historically, Singapore has undergone various stages of economic restructuring as it moved up the ladder of comparative advantage. While in the earlier phase of growth, foreign direct investment played a central role in providing the technology to move up the ladder of comparative advantage, the next phase of growth is likely to be characterised by small and medium-sized enterprises playing a more vital role in contributing to the sources of productivity growth. The process of economic restructuring to boost productivity of small and medium-sized enterprises by helping them improve management practices and selling into overseas markets will contribute to overall productivity growth. Since it is in the nature of many startups to fail, the pace of job destruction might pick up.[2] This is on top of major technological shifts that displace jobs characterised by routine tasks. To keep the unemployment rate low, it is necessary

---

[1]See Edward P. Lazear and Kristin McCue, 2017, "Hires and Separations in Equilibrium," NBER Working Paper No. 23059.

[2]See Tor Jakob Klette and Samuel Kortum, 2004, "Innovating Firms and Aggregate Innovation," *Journal of Political Economy*, 112(5): 986–1018. Among the list of stylised facts, Klette and Kortum note that while smaller firms have a lower probability of survival, those that do survive tend to grow faster than larger firms.

to create an environment in which there is an increased pace of new firm creation so that, even as workers lose their jobs from businesses that fail, new job vacancies are simultaneously created.

A feature of the modern economy is that of relationship specificity between economic units, which is that some or all of the economic value within a relationship, such as that between a financier and an entrepreneur or that between an entrepreneur and a worker, is lost when the economic units break up. In other words, there is positive economic surplus when two economic units enter into a collaborative arrangement.[3] The output produced through the collaboration exceeds the sum of the ex post opportunity cost of each economic unit should the relationship break up. Since contracts are incomplete, it is possible for one or both of the economic units within the relationship to hold up the other. This possibility of opportunistic behaviour means that each economic unit will enter into a collaborative relationship with another only if it is assured that the reward that it can expect to earn is at least equal to what it can earn ex ante. Depending on the bargaining strength of each economic unit, the reward to each economic unit includes a share of the economic surplus. In general equilibrium, the less specific factor ends up with a segmented factor market. For example, in the early days of Singapore's economic development, foreign capital placed in Singapore could be held up by striking workers. Since foreign capital could be invested elsewhere to earn the world interest rate if it were not committed to building a plant in Singapore, the owners of foreign capital limited the number of workers they employed, leaving more people to work in the secondary labour market. The multinational firms in Singapore paid a wage premium to a rationed workforce, leaving many others to take on jobs with lower pay.

The problem of holdup would become more important in the relationship between financiers and entrepreneurs in the next stage of Singapore's economic development as new startups need financing from angel investors and venture capitalists. The distinction between

---

[3]See Ricardo Caballero, 2007, *Specificity and the Macroeconomics of Restructuring*, Cambridge, MA: MIT Press.

firm-specific and general training will also play an important role in the future economy as the digital revolution makes many jobs redundant even as it creates new job tasks.

Capital and Labour

If a machine that is put to use in the production of a good in cooperation with labour could be dismantled and put to use to work with labour to produce a different good when the production of the first good is no longer profitable, then, barring normal wear and tear, each unit of capital would be paid according to the value of its marginal product. Similarly, if a worker who loses his job in one industry can readily pack up and move to another job in another industry the next instant, each worker would be paid according to the value of its marginal product. The market economy would be efficient. However, for technological reasons, sometimes capital that has been customised for use in one industry cannot be reused in another industry. For example, a machine used in a bakery cannot be easily retrofitted for use in the marine industry. In such a situation, a steady push for higher wages could initially result in a steady increase in wage share. In the longer term, however, incentives are created for labour-replacing technological change, which could reverse the initial rise of the wage share.[4]

In the new economy, it is likely that workers' skills are not readily transferable across industries. If a worker loses a job in one industry, he might not have the skill to immediately be productive in a job in a new industry. This situation poses a special challenge in a labour-scarce economy since new startups might not readily find the workers with the desired skills even as workers who lose their jobs remain unemployed.

Capital and labour specificity can arise not simply from techno-logical reasons. When a unit of capital meets a worker to form a collaborative enterprise, not all possible states of the world can be

---

[4]Ricardo Caballero, *op cit.*, offers this as an explanation for the rise of French unemployment from the late 1970s.

enumerated to be put into a contract that would regulate their working relationship. Since the court cannot enforce complete contracts, there is the possibility of opportunistic behaviour. While in the early days of Singapore's economic development, it might be thought that capital was the more specific factor and had better alternatives before entering into a collaborative relationship, the situation now might be characterised as one in which labour has better alternatives in a labour-scarce economy. The result is that entrepreneurs looking for workers might find it difficult to fill in job slots. Automation will help these startups perform certain functions without a heavy reliance on workers. Instead, more engaging tasks can be given to workers who will find their work more challenging and engaging. In this way, more promising businesses can be successfully launched.

Entrepreneurs and Financiers

Multinational companies bring in their own capital to work with workers to produce their output. As new business startups drive innovation in the new economy, a central relationship that comes into focus is that of financiers and entrepreneurs. Angel investors provide financing for startups. As the education system invests in providing students with the opportunity to venture into the unknown and increase the supply of entrepreneurs, the match between angel investors and people with good business ideas might improve. This would improve the expected returns to financiers and increase the number of startups that receive financing. More successful early-stage business ventures might then stimulate the supply of financing from venture capitalists.

As Singapore seeks to develop an environment conducive to innovative activities, the digital revolution is also making it possible to devise alternative means of making payments. There are benefits to developing the financial sector. Financial intermediation arises to provide a means for diversification and a means to minimise monitoring costs.[5] The formal banking sector can contribute to financing

---

[5]See Bruce Champ, Scott Freeman and Joseph Haslag, 2016, *Modeling Monetary Economies*, 4th edition, New York: Cambridge University Press.

innovative projects. However, it is likely that the supply of funds for business startups will come from the development of the venture capital industry.[6] Suppose that you as a financier own a stock of capital k. You want to lend your capital to entrepreneurs. A business project requires a minimum amount of capital. You would want to diversify your risk so you won't put all your capital into one project. You choose more than one project to diversify your risk, with the exact number of projects you choose depending on how risk averse you are. Each business venture carries a risk that it may fail, yet the exact circumstances under which it fails cannot be written into a financial contract. In such an incomplete contracts framework, the financier cares about the allocation of control rights such as board rights, voting rights, and liquidation rights. If the entrepreneur fails to deliver a minimum level of financial and non-financial performance, the financier exercises his control rights. However, if the business venture is performing well, the financier exercises only his cash-flow rights but relinquishes most of his control and liquidation rights.[7]

Since a project requires a minimum amount of capital to start and each investor divides his capital among all the projects, the entrepreneur needs to raise capital from more than one investor. Suppose that there is a well-functioning financial system that intermediates between financiers and entrepreneurs. With funds pooled together, several venture capital firms make loans to each entrepreneur. Although each loan given to an entrepreneur is risky, the diversification of the loan portfolio by the financial system means that it gets the average rate of return on its loans. The expected

---

[6]The Monetary Authority of Singapore (MAS) announced on 20 October 2017 a simplified regulatory regime for managers of venture capital following public consultation. Among other things, the new regulatory regime simplifies and shortens the authorisation process for venture capital managers with MAS focusing primarily on existing fit and proper and anti-money laundering safeguards. See MAS press release titled "MAS simplifies rules for managers of venture capital funds to facilitate start-ups' access to capital" (20 October 2017).

[7]See Steven N. Kaplan and Per Strömberg, 2003, "Financial Contracting Theory Meets the Real World: An Empirical Analysis of Venture Capital Contracts," *Review of Economic Studies*, 70(2): 281–315.

return to a project is higher with a fully-functioning financial system. Similarly, the expected rate of return per unit of capital is also higher than without the fully-functioning financial system.

If there is free entry into the business of financial intermediation, what each financial firm pays, in competitive equilibrium, to a saver is greater than what is earned without a fully-functioning financial system. The competitive financial system achieves a higher expected rate of return to financing business projects by economizing on monitoring costs to increase the chances that a new business startup will succeed. Going forward, the development of the financial system that facilitates the financing of new business ventures will play a critical role in boosting indigenous innovation. As the economy develops greater depth and experience in having new business ideas tested, with monitoring of each step of the project carefully evaluated before the next tranche of financing is given, Singapore can see herself becoming attractive to major venture capital firms.

Firm-specific and General Training

Would a firm pay for a worker's general training? In a competitive labour market, there would be little incentive for a firm to invest in a worker's general training. Suppose that firm A chooses to pay for a worker's training to acquire a skill that is usable also at other firms. After the firm has incurred the investment cost, and the worker now has acquired a higher level of skill that other firms also find valuable, the other firms can then offer to pay the worker more without incurring the original costs of training. Anticipating this, no firm would want to pay for their workers' general training. An exception would be if, despite the general training, the firm has some degree of monopsony power due to superior information about its current employees so that it is able to bid down the wage to below the worker's value of marginal product. This might provide firms with some incentive to provide general training to their workers.[8]

---

[8]See Daron Acemoglu and Jorn-Steffen Pischke, 1998, "Why Do Firms Train? Theory and Evidence," *Quarterly Journal of Economics*, 113(1): 79–119.

While each small and medium-sized enterprise might not find it profitable to pay for general training, an industry consortium might find it profitable to provide general training at an industry level. Such workers have skills that can be most profitably employed within the industry so firms within the industry can recoup their investment in the general training.

On the other hand, a firm and its worker might be willing to share in the investment cost of firm-specific training. In part, this cost sharing could be achieved by the worker accepting a pay rate which is a little lower than the value of its marginal product after the training for a period of time. If a firm bears the full cost of the firm-specific training, it faces the possibility of suffering a loss on its investment if the employee quits after he has been trained. To deter its workers from quitting after receiving the training, the human resource department might devise a wage policy to induce its trained employees to remain at the firm. By raising the pay scale above the market rate, it seeks to make its employee face a penalty if he quits. However, as all firms think likewise, the economy-wide pay rate is driven to above its market-clearing level. Consequently, there is job rationing and a pool of involuntarily unemployed workers is created. Other forms of arrangements might be made to make it profitable for firms to provide firm-specific training such as requiring workers to serve a one-year bond after training. Creating a good working environment also helps to encourage workers' loyalty to the firms that provide them the firm-specific training. Since there are social costs to having long-term unemployment, there is also a case for the government to provide employment and training subsidies to firms.

Chapter 8

Role of Government

The United States and the European Union have responded to widening wage gaps in very different ways, leading to two different outcomes. The EU has chosen to spend big amounts of public resources to provide generous unemployment benefits. Jobs are also made more stable through legislation which makes firing difficult. Paradoxically, however, making firing more difficult leads firms to be more hesitant about hiring. The U.S., on the other hand, has less strict hire-and-fire rules as well as more flexible wages. The result, it is argued, is a much lower average rate of unemployment. It should be pointed out, however, that a more disaggregated breakdown of unemployment rates by education categories shows that the unemployment rate for the less skilled in the U.S. is much higher than for the skilled, and has been rising since the early 1970s. Moreover, the low wages of the unskilled — relative to the value of leisure and to what could be earned in the underground economy and in illegal activities — makes working not worthwhile so that the "non-employment rate" has been high among the less skilled in the U.S. The challenge for Singapore's policy-makers is that they must determine what approach to adopt in providing a form of insurance to less-skilled workers in the face of loss of incomes. The nature of the social safety nets that Singapore chooses to develop will be vitally important as the provision of insurance needs to take into account its effect on private incentives and be fiscally sustainable. To continue to be integrated into the global economy requires the means to fight recessions while retaining fiscal sustainability. There is also a role that the government should still play in facilitating innovation even though widespread innovative activities have to come from the grassroots. Since economic restructuring involves many small firms, there are activities that enjoy economies of scale mainly at the industry and national level. Government intervention helps to generate benefits enjoyed by all firms.

Redistribution

The design of social safety nets represents society's effort to provide social insurance. At a fundamental level, we recognise that some negative events occur in an individual's life that are unforseen and, to a certain degree, beyond his or her ability to control: falling seriously ill, outliving one's lifetime resources, losing a job, and suffering a physical disability. To provide protection to its citizens against such contingent events, one might think that we could rely solely on private insurance companies. The argument is that risk averse individuals would find it in their own self-interest to purchase insurance policies that are offered at actuarially fair prices. However, because of asymmetric information problems — one side of the market has private information not readily available to the other side — leading to adverse selection and moral hazard, full insurance is generally not available. Thus, there is a role for the provision of social insurance. In contrast to private insurance where purchases are entirely voluntary, the provision of social insurance involves some degree of compulsion through application of the law.[1] The practical challenge in the design of a scheme for provision of social insurance is that the presence of adverse selection and moral hazard plaguing a private insurance market still has to be confronted. Providing protection without sufficiently attenuating the presence of adverse selection and moral hazard leads to fiscal unsustainability. Another point is that the provision of insurance relies on risk diversification based on the law of large numbers. Yet, there are aggregate shocks

---

[1]See Martin Feldstein, 2005, "Rethinking Social Insurance," *American Economic Review*, 95(1): 1–24.

that a country might face, such as a prolonged recession that leads to an unusually large pool of long-term unemployed, that a social insurance system cannot handle without further policy intervention such as employment and training subsidies.

There are broadly two different approaches to financing social insurance: a defined benefit system and a defined contribution system. In a defined benefit system, payroll taxes are collected from the working young to finance the benefits received by the retired old. In an overlapping-generations economy, a worker's payroll tax can be interpreted as his "forced saving", which earns a return that depends positively on the rate of population growth. That rate of return is high when the entry rate of the working young into the economy is high so that there are more working young to support a retired old. A slowdown in population growth, resulting from a declining fertility rate and immigration rate, leads to a decline in the old-age support ratio putting pressure to either raise the payroll tax rate or reduce the benefits for *fiscal sustainability*.

A defined contribution scheme such as Singapore's Central Provident Fund (CPF), on the other hand, legislates that a percentage of the worker's pay, call it the employee's contribution, goes to a fund. There is a matching contribution by the employer, call it the employer's contribution, to the fund credited to the worker's account.[2] The fund is then invested, with the compulsory savings earning an annual return based upon the performance of the fund. Notice that with a defined contribution scheme, the fiscal sustainability of the scheme is not directly related to demographics such as an ageing population. Demographics have an impact only insofar as it affects the capital market, which in turn affects the fund's portfolio performance. With a given percentage contribution rate, the size of a worker's account grows annually with the rising wage profile.

---

[2]It is a standard result in public economics that the true incidence of the mandated contribution depends on the elasticities of labour supply and labour demand and does not depend on whether it is the employer or the employee who makes the contribution.

Social security systems, also known as national pension plans, have their roots in Europe in the 19th century.[3] In the 20th century, they grew in scale. The U.S. social security system was introduced in 1935 as the economy emerged from the debilitating effects of the Great Depression. If workers have time-consistent preferences and there is an actuarially fair annuity market, there might not need to be compulsory savings for retirement. However, there is strong evidence that many people have what are called quasi-hyperbolic time preferences or self-control problems, which lead to undersaving.[4] Forcing them to make contributions to a mandatory social security system is a good way to ensure they have money set aside for the future. Enrolling everyone may also be seen as a way of ensuring taxes will not have to be raised to finance the cost of taking care of the elderly who have opted out of the scheme, and thus do not have adequate assets to finance their retirement needs. Such a social security system, with its universal coverage, therefore helps people save for the future.

Most national pension plans in Western economies, however, operate on a pay-as-you-go basis. In other words, social security taxes collected from working young people are used to finance the retirement benefits of the old. There is also a social equity element in these public pension plans. A person who is born into a less well-to-do family, lacking the resources to get a head start in life, gets a boost in his retirement income. This is because there is typically a degree of progressivity in retirement benefits, so that a low-wage worker receives more in benefits in percentage terms compared with his wage earnings. Recipients also collect benefits for as long as they are alive. This means that the system absorbs the cost of increased longevity.

How does the CPF system compare on the issue of social equity? With the Workfare Income Supplement scheme, low-wage workers who are employed receive payouts that augment their CPF balances

---

[3]My discussion of social security systems draws on Hian Teck Hoon, 2014, "Why CPF-style Systems Generally Work Better," *The Straits Times* (2 July).

[4]See Richard H. Thaler, 2015, *Misbehaving: The Making of Behavioral Economics*, New York: W. W. Norton & Company.

and contribute to their retirement incomes. High-wage earners do not enjoy this benefit. Instead, CPF members with adequate balances are obliged to participate in CPF Life, a national annuity scheme that allows older members to receive a monthly income for life. The only exceptions are for those with private annuities or pension plans that pay higher benefits. The scheme allows risk pooling and avoids the problem of adverse selection. CPF Life also goes some way towards providing insurance for increased longevity.

The CPF system has important macroeconomic effects. In 2016, CPF balances due to members (net of withdrawals) stood at $329 billion, making up close to 30 percent of total financial assets of the household sector, not including residential property assets.[5] Together with a generally prudent fiscal policy over the years, Singapore has built up a net creditor position relative to the rest of the world. Its strong reserves position gives it an advantage during international financial crises. Many Western economies introduced a pay-as-you-go social security system at a time when their economies were growing rapidly and their populations were relatively young. With ageing populations, these pension plans are placing a strain on national budgets. Although a move to introduce a CPF-style contribution system has been debated in these countries, there is still the problem of how to finance the needs of the transitional generation of elderly people. That generation paid taxes to help finance the social security system when they were young. But no money was set aside by the authorities to finance social security benefits during the transition to a CPF-style system of individual accounts. As the population ages, Singapore also faces the challenge of providing retirement adequacy for CPF members. But the problems facing the CPF system are not as serious because they do not have as much impact on the national budget.

If the CPF is to serve as a means of helping its members save for their retirement years, no more flexibility in the way the funds are now being used should be given. Moreover, if the CPF is also needed

---

[5]Department of Statistics, Singapore Ministry of Trade and Industry, *Yearbook of Statistics Singapore*, 2017.

to provide medical insurance cover, then mandatory participation in the national annuity scheme is justified. The Government can absorb the risk of investing CPF funds because of its greater financial depth and capacity to tax. But the provision of adequate funds to finance an ageing population of Singaporeans depends more fundamentally on the ability of the country to maintain its economic dynamism, as the economy transits from an era of catch-up growth to being a mature economy.

To provide lifelong medical insurance coverage, it is necessary that during working life, a worker makes contributions into his Medical Account. Each worker's Medical Account can be drawn upon to pay his insurance premiums for policies to cover hospitalisation and catastrophic illnesses. The healthcare providers can adjust premiums based on age but cannot reject an application based on existing health conditions. Correspondingly, the purchase of these insurance policies is compulsory for all workers.[6] The reason for making it compulsory for all workers to purchase these insurance policies is to avoid letting the *adverse selection problem* cause it to be unprofitable for any company to offer health insurance as the healthier choose to opt out. To contain the costs of health insurance, there would typically be a deductible and a positive coinsurance rate that come along with an insurance policy, which would require a trade-off between providing protection and tackling the incentive to overspend once a person is insured.[7]

---

[6] A public mandate is applied in the Affordable Care Act in the U.S. In Singapore, the government announced in August 2013 that it would modify a national health insurance programme, called Medishield, which excluded pre-existing medical conditions and allowed an opt-out option, to cover pre-existing medical conditions and to require everyone to participate. This scheme is currently run under the name Medishield Life. For an economic analysis of the use of a public mandate, see Lawrence Summers, 1989, "Some Simple Economics of Mandated Benefits," *American Economic Review: Papers and Proceedings*, 79(2): 177–183.

[7] See Kenneth Arrow, 1985, "Theoretical Issues in Health Insurance," in *Collected Papers of Kenneth J. Arrow: Applied Economics*, Cambridge, MA: Harvard University Press. See also, Kenneth Arrow, 1963, "Uncertainty and the Welfare Economics of Medical Care," *American Economic Review*, 53(5): 941–973 for an early analysis of adverse selection and moral hazard in the context of the medical care industry.

What about unemployment insurance? The *moral hazard problem* makes it not viable for private companies to sell unemployment insurance policies. One feature of employment determination, that is of relevance when thinking about the design of unemployment insurance, concerns the job search behaviour of workers. When a firm lays off its workers due either to a seasonal business downturn or to a worsened economic outlook, the affected workers are left without an earning during the period of unemployment. Since the economy is one in which there are job vacancies even when there are concurrently unemployed workers, it is often thought that the intensity of job search on the part of the unemployed and the value of his reservation wage both affect the expected duration of unemployment. The more intensely he searches for a job and the lower his reservation wage, the shorter is the expected duration of unemployment. How does the introduction of an unemployment benefit affect the worker's search behaviour?[8] One channel through which the introduction of an unemployment benefit affects the worker's behaviour is to cause him to substitute towards being in the state of "remaining unemployed" since it is less costly to be without a job — a substitution effect. (This effect is also referred to as a moral hazard effect.) From society's point of view, this distortion in the worker's incentive to prolong his unemployment duration incurs a deadweight loss.

There may, however, be a second effect — a liquidity effect — that is distinct from the substitution effect of introducing an unemployment benefit. Given that the credit market is imperfect so that it is not always possible to borrow against future incomes, some workers who lose their jobs must substantially cut back on their consumption. Certain financial obligations like paying for their children's education might not be met. For liquidity-constrained workers, the loss of a job can have debilitating effects not only

---

[8] A typical range of values of estimated elasticity of unemployment duration with respect to unemployment benefits in the U.S. is 0.4 to 0.8, that is, a 10 percent increase in unemployment benefits leads to 4–8 percent increase in the average duration of unemployment. This is cited in Raj Chetty, 2008, "Moral Hazard vs Liquidity and Optimal Unemployment Insurance," *Journal of Political Economy*, 116(2): 173–234.

on themselves but also on their family members. The economist Raj Chetty finds that, in the U.S., 60 percent of the increase in unemployment duration resulting from the increase in unemployment insurance benefits is due to the liquidity effect.[9] Given the existing system of unemployment insurance in the U.S. that pays a constant unemployment benefit for six months, Chetty finds a replacement rate equal to 50 percent of the pre-unemployment wage is close to optimal.

A national unemployment insurance scheme can be organised as follows: Firms are required to pay experience-rated payroll taxes into a national insurance fund, that is, the amount of payroll taxes a firm has to pay depends positively upon the number of workers it has previously laid off.[10] However, as there is typically a maximum amount that firms have to pay, it has been argued that firms have an incentive to lay off too many workers and then recalling them later when the unemployment benefit payout ends. It has also been pointed out that there is often a spike in the number of unemployed who take up jobs round about the time that the unemployment benefit payout ceases suggesting that workers have a greater incentive to turn down a job with an unemployment insurance scheme.

Long-term unemployment sparked by a prolonged recession can lead to the loss of skills and dislocation from regular networks that make reintegrating into the job market far more difficult. Government efforts to build up a pool of firms that are ready to hire and train a retrenched worker or one who has been unemployed for several months through giving the participating firms employment and training subsidies can help to reduce long-term unemployment. Without a national unemployment insurance scheme in place, workers would have to provide self-insurance — saving when they are employed — to provide financial resources to tide through those few months before they are matched to a suitable job.

---

[9]See Chetty (2008).

[10]For a proposal on an unemployment insurance savings account in the U.S. context, see Martin Feldstein and Daniel Altman, 2007, "Unemployment Insurance Savings Account," in James Poterba (ed.) *Tax Policy and the Economy*, Vol. 21, May, Cambridge, MA: MIT Press, pp. 35–63.

Stabilisation

Since most of the decline in Singapore's unemployment beginning from 1965 onwards is structural in nature — excepting, perhaps, the rise in unemployment in 1986, 2003 and 2009 that have large cyclical components — it can be argued that most of the fiscal surpluses have also been structural in nature. A major reason for such structural surpluses was that as a country Singapore was able to do things that produced exceptional growth, that is, growth that far exceeded what we or anyone else could have anticipated. At given tax rates, and no corresponding proportionate increases in government spending, we were able to generate fiscal surpluses. Thus, whether Singapore could hope to continue generating fiscal surpluses would depend on whether Singapore could maintain the capacity to produce exceptional growth which, in this next phase of development, would require two things: (a) institutions to generate economic dynamism; and (b) the ability to maintain social cohesion.

There is a good rationale for maintaining fiscal surpluses. Surpluses are needed to build resilience against shocks which come along with our open economy and integration with global capital markets such as currency crises. There appears to be strong evidence of nominal wage rigidity.[11] Given nominal wage stickiness, the short-run aggregate supply curve is not vertical but possesses a positive slope. A jobs credit, by lowering the firm's unit labor cost, makes possible the firm's supply of an initial output level at a more competitive price at given exchange rate.[12] The improved international competitiveness made possible by the jobs credit serves to expand aggregate demand by boosting exports.[13] By expanding aggregate demand, a jobs credit helps to remove the constraint on firm hiring due to limited sales.

---

[11] See Mary Daly, Bart Hobijn, and Brian Lucking, 2012, "Why Has Wage Growth Stayed Strong?" Federal Reserve Bank of San Francisco *Economic Letter*, April 2.

[12] In other words, given nominal wage stickiness, a jobs credit shifts the positively-sloped aggregate supply curve to the right along a negatively-sloped aggregate demand curve.

[13] There is also a real balance effect that causes a stimulus to aggregate demand as the lower domestic price raises the real purchasing power of money and boosts spending.

A jobs credit also alleviates cash-flow problems for recession-hit firms and prevents more lay-offs from happening. Since there is a strong case to generate strong economic recoveries when hit by a recessionary shock so that workers are not caught up in long-term unemployment, the country needs to generate surpluses that can be drawn upon to finance jobs credits. Having the fiscal resources to keep recessions short is important as the resulting macroeconomic stability enables innovative startups to compete in developing new and better-quality products. Firms can also better assess the performance of their workers and tie pay to their performance.

Allocation

Over the medium to long term, the economy tends towards its potential output or long-run aggregate supply.[14] Although the late British economist John Maynard Keynes famously said that in the long run we are all dead, it is in fact our ability to produce a relentless rise in potential output that explains Singapore's dramatic rise in the standard of living within a generation. Looking ahead, it is still going to be our ability to create the right conditions for potential output to grow that will ensure a good and steady supply of challenging jobs with rewarding pay.

Countries gain from specialisation based upon comparative advantage. A nation's comparative advantage, however, is not static. Rather, it is dynamic and it changes over time as a result of past investment in physical and human capital as well as in knowledge creation. Recent research also shows that a nation's economic culture and institutions are important determinants of a country's comparative advantage. Singapore can build upon its reputation of a business-friendly environment, having strong intellectual property protection, and an education system geared towards training venturesome and entrepreneurial individuals to attract new business activities here.

---

[14]My discussion in this section draws on my article published in *The Business Times* on 9 June 2009 titled "Mapping Out S'pore's Economic Strategies".

Countries transit from a phase of catch-up growth to that of steady-state growth as they become mature economies. During the phase of catch-up growth, countries grow at a much more rapid pace than the global economic leaders. This is, after all, how poorer nations catch up with the richer economies. China, India and Vietnam come readily to mind as countries that are currently undergoing this phase of growth. Singapore, most likely, has reached the mature phase of growth. At this second stage of growth, the fuel that will drive economic prosperity and generate challenging jobs is innovation rather than capital accumulation. Singapore's increase in research and development spending as well as its efforts to attract top scientists and researchers to the city-state to live and work will help us make the transition from being technology followers to being technology leaders. Small and medium-sized enterprises play a complementary role to large firms in the innovation process. Our country not only requires scientific breakthroughs in the laboratory. The type of innovation that percolates through a dynamic economy also comes from the testing of ideas by businesses in the marketplace. As the economist Edmund Phelps has emphasised, a capitalist economy such as Singapore is fraught with novelty, ambiguity and uncertainty because its firms have no way of knowing beforehand how the new products that are launched will be well-received by potential customers. In such an environment, small firms financed by venture capitalists and angel investors have an advantage over large firms since they are more ready to try out new things. Large established firms, on the other hand, have an advantage in dealing with well-tested products that require huge capital expenditures.

The government has an important role to play to foster economic inclusion and support economic dynamism. Although creative ideas for business ventures must come from the grassroots, the government can provide support for industry-level initiatives for training in areas such as good management practices and establishment of export platforms for small and medium-sized firms to venture overseas. To ensure that there continues to be public support for integration into the global economy, economic prosperity also needs to be widely shared. Since globalisation and the capitalist system tend to generate income inequalities, schemes to bolster the pay and employability of low-wage workers, such as the Workfare Income Supplement scheme, are needed. Since the economy is also vulnerable to adverse external shocks that can cause GDP to fall below the potential level, the government needs to generate fiscal surpluses in good times in order to finance counter-recessionary measures in bad times. The global economy offers both opportunities and threats. We can look back at how the country has faced and surmounted past difficulties. It also must have guiding principles to provide moorings.

Chapter 9

Social Cohesion and Political Equilibrium

The steady expansion of the economic pie, not only the total size, but on a per capita basis, facilitated the achievement of social cohesion during Singapore's catch-up phase of growth as gains were broadly shared across the population. A commitment to be engaged in the global economy through the international flow of goods and services, capital, and people found broad public support. As a mature economy, Singapore's pace of growth is determined by the rate of indigenous innovation and the pace of advance of frontier technology. The Romer and Schumpeterian models of endogenous technological change provide the microeconomic underpinnings for growth of the world's technology frontier.[1] In practice, the bulk of the world's R&D is carried out by the G-5 countries: France, Germany (West Germany until 1990), Japan, the United Kingdom, and the United States. We can call them the "frontier economies". The endogenous growth models developed by the economists Paul Romer, Philippe Aghion and Peter Howitt explain the factors and mechanisms behind the determinants of the growth rate of frontier technology, driven by the frontier economies. With the end of catch-up growth, as Singapore gets closer to the technology frontier, successful business ventures that launch new and higher-quality products enable Singapore to join the ranks of these frontier economies. Whereas in the past,

---

[1]Philippe Aghion and Peter Howitt, 2009, *The Economics of Growth*, Cambridge, MA: MIT Press.

a transition from being a relatively poor country to one that was getting closer to the standard of living of developed economies fostered a sense of social cohesion, in future, it will be the ability to create an economic system that supports innovative activities that provides the social glue.

When we ask why some countries are rich while others are poor, our answer is that rich countries invest more in capital, spend more time in formal schooling, devote more time to acquire the skills needed to apply technology developed by the frontier economies, and are able to generate a greater amount of output from given inputs (that is, they have higher TFP). However, this answer prompts one to ask the further question: Why is it that some countries invest more than others, and individuals in some economies spend more time learning how to use new technologies? It can be argued that it is not geography or culture that provides the answer to the deeper question. Instead, it is the quality of the *social infrastructure* of an economy — the rules and regulations and the institutions that enforce them — that is a primary determinant of the extent to which individuals are willing to make the long-term investments in capital, skills, and technology that are associated with long-run economic success. As examples, we can think of economic well-being between citizens of North Korea and South Korea and citizens of East Germany and West Germany before the fall of Berlin Wall. In both examples, the populations involved shared similar geography and culture but had different economic and political institutions that clearly drove their people towards achieving or not achieving growth.[2] Singapore's political institutions will have to support a new phase of Singapore's growth that will be characterised by a faster pace of creative destruction.

Allocation of Talent

There is currently no "canonical" model to help us think about which institutions are the most important and how they act to

---

[2]Daron Acemoglu and James Robinson, 2012, *Why Nations Fail: The Origins of Power, Prosperity, and Poverty*, New York: Crown Publishing.

influence people's incentives. Nevertheless, we can think about the problem in an analogous manner to how a manager of a multinational corporation decides whether to undertake an investment by opening a subsidiary in a foreign country.[3] The manager conducts a cost-benefit analysis. Suppose that launching the business subsidiary in the foreign country involves a one-time setup cost. Once the business is set up, let's assume that it generates a profit every year that the business remains open. The expected present discounted value of the stream of profits is the value of the business subsidiary once it has been set up. With this formulation of the problem, deciding whether or not to undertake the project proceeds as follows: If the expected present discounted value of the stream of profits exceeds the one-time setup cost, then the business subsidiary is set up. The same cost-benefit analysis can be applied to whether an investment in capital is undertaken or whether an individual decides whether to spend another year in school.

What determines the magnitudes of the one-time setup cost and the expected present discounted value of the stream of profits in various countries around the world? Is there sufficient variation in these to explain the enormous variation in investment rates, educational attainment, and TFP? There is, indeed, a great deal of variation in the costs of setting up a business and in the ability of investors to reap returns from their investments. Such variation arises in large part from differences in government policies and institutions or social infrastructure.[4] A good government provides the institutions and social infrastructure that minimise the one-time setup cost and maximise the expected present discounted value of the stream of profits, thereby encouraging investment and startups that launch new and better-quality products.

There is empirical evidence to show positive *correlations* between the index of the quality of social infrastructure and investment rates,

[3] Jones and Vollrath, *op cit.*
[4] Robert E. Hall and Charles I. Jones, 1999, "Why Do Some Countries Produce So Much More Output per Worker than Others?" *Quarterly Journal of Economics*, 114(1): 83–116.

skill accumulation, and TFP, respectively.[5] There is further work by economists who use "natural experiments" to provide evidence that good social infrastructure is not only positively correlated to higher investment, skill accumulation, and TFP but, in fact, is a *cause* of the latter.[6] Turning to the question of "growth miracles", we might ask, "How is it that some countries such as Singapore, Hong Kong, and Japan can move from being relatively poor to being relatively rich over a span of time as short as forty years?" Similarly, how is it that an economy like Argentina's and Venezuela's can make the reverse move? The answer is that basic changes in the social infrastructure of the economy led to growth miracles in the former and growth disasters in the latter.

Singapore has now reached a mature phase of its economic development. To retain economic prosperity, it needs to create the right incentive for talent to be engaged in productive economic activity, both through the public sector in an enabling role as well as in direct economic activity and to find a means of selecting political leaders.[7] Sustaining a high-quality public sector (defined broadly to include both the government and administrative sector) remains of high priority in the face of challenges posed by globalisation. There remains the need for good institutions to foster an entrepreneurial and innovative environment, and for effective political leadership. Yet, the possibility of earning very much more in the private sector creates a big problem for personnel retention in the public sector. The government has sought to address this problem by tying public sector pay to private sector pay, but there are dissenters. Greater mobility of talented people between the private and public sectors — demonstrating that they have skills that are valued in both sectors — will help to increase the public's receptivity to this form of remuneration. Recruiting and retaining public sector talent is a

---

[5]Hall and Jones, *op cit.*

[6]Daron Acemoglu, Simon Johnson and James Robinson, 2005, "Institutions as the Fundamental Cause of Long-run Growth," in *Handbook of Economic Growth*, Volume 1A, Philippe Aghion and Steven Durlauf (eds.), Amsterdam: Elsevier.

[7]See Timothy Besley, 2006, *Principled Agents? The Political Economy of Good Government*, Oxford: Oxford University Press.

crucial ingredient in establishing an effective social infrastructure. It remains as important for economic progress today as in the past, but it is increasingly more difficult in a winner-takes-all society.

We have also noted that whereas market forces and technology in the first three-and-a-half decades acted to narrow the wage gap, they are now likely to widen wage inequality. This means that policy interventions in the form of further wage income supplements will be required to boost the take-home pay of low-wage workers, and employment and training subsidies will be required to help match and retrain workers who lose their jobs. As market forces act to shift wage gains disproportionately towards high-skill workers, there is a case for an increase in top marginal tax rates to finance social interventions to foster economic inclusion and achieve social cohesion.

Tripartism

The ability of labour and business enterprises to resolve conflicts will also be vital for the future. Two key institutions have played central roles in helping Singapore resolve conflicts when hit by major adverse economic shocks. These are the Central Provident Fund (CPF) and the National Wages Council (NWC). A major negative shock affecting the whole economy requires that some sacrifice be made — if real wages are largely maintained, jobs must inevitably be lost as firms seek to keep their bottom lines healthy. In the end, to fight the sharp 1985–86 recession, real wage cuts were achieved through substantial cuts in the CPF rate thus avoiding massive job losses. It is conceivable that uniform cuts in the CPF rate are easier to achieve when workers' wages are equitable than when they are very unequal. The shorter job tenure of particular jobs, the increased use of stock options as a form of compensation, as well as an increasing number of individuals who are self-employed, will limit the government's ability to use adjustments of the CPF rate as a macroeconomic tool. To fight the 2009 recession, the jobs credits were funded by drawing on reserves. After the economy strongly rebounded in 2010, the money was subsequently returned in 2011. To fund future jobs credits, the government has to build fiscal surpluses when the economy is doing well so that they have the fiscal resources to fight recessions.

As an alternative to implementing major wage cuts, the government has sought to make wages more flexible; a monthly variable component is to be adjusted in the light of business conditions. But wage cuts — even of the variable kind — hurt workers' morale; each firm may reason that cutting workers' pay will reduce productivity, which will actually decrease profits by more than the cost savings. This behaviour on the part of firms tends to build into the economy a downward rigidity of aggregate wages. The reality is that a small, highly open economy like Singapore has a limited range of other macroeconomic tools. The openness to international flows of capital essentially makes monetary policy ineffective. So the room to manoeuvre is quite limited. The tripartite partners can strengthen a system in which the economy is flexible and able to quickly retrain workers so that, in the face of creative destruction, new jobs are constantly being created.

Inter-temporal Preferences

In the phase of catch-up growth that began in 1965, the initial low standard of living tended to make the immediate satisfying of basic needs very important. However, once the economy started on a path of catch-up growth, the imagination of higher living standards in the future enabled citizens to forgo current pleasures to invest in acquiring personal skills and developing the human capital of their children. The ability to imagine the future helped them become more patient, that is, to have a low rate of time preference. Having a low rate of time preference is important to achieve good equilibrium outcomes. The high rate of investment led to capital deepening, which bolstered their productivity and therefore their pay. The willingness to go for retraining to acquire new skills as the economy moved up along the ladder of comparative advantage also enabled workers to enjoy a growing wage profile over time. The expectation of steady growth in wage earnings acted to help people imagine a better future.

At given individual rates of time preference, the fact that growth was rapid made the arrival of future benefits appear relatively sooner. In a sense, a growth slowdown with the end of catch-up growth would make future benefits appear to arrive later. In many situations involving interpersonal interactions, it is the ability to give greater weight to future benefits in the calculation of personal benefits that results in choosing actions that lead to higher welfare for everyone in society. When workers in the next phase of development look towards a career with more job disruptions, this can tend to weaken their personal incentive to defer consumption and make current investments in acquiring new skills. Creating an economic system that will take advantage of new opportunities to develop indigenous innovation and to develop a social safety net that will enable people to quickly find new employment when they lose their jobs will help to generate optimism among citizens. The ability to imagine the future together helps to generate actions that would boost cooperation among citizens to obtain a better outcome for all.

Part III

Achieving Economic Justice

Chapter 10

Pitfalls, Fundamentals, and Choices

There are pitfalls to avoid such as continuing to expect that the economy's standard of living will continue to grow at the rate that it did during the catch-up phase. Such expectations, if built into workers' view of their wage prospects, would translate into higher unemployment. There are also fundamental forces at work to deliver an economy that is rich, and yet deliver good jobs and pay. Maintaining economic openness enables the economy to achieve economic dynamism so as to create the resources to achieve economic inclusion. Finally, there are choices to be made that are related to the challenges facing the Singapore economy.

As the economy enters the next phase of its economic development, it faces another set of challenges. How to transit from catch-up growth arising from technological diffusion from frontier economies to generating indigenous innovation?[1] How to face the problem of a shrinking local workforce? How to manage a shift in job preferences with rising wealth and educational attainments? How to cope with disruption arising from automation, robotisation and artificial intelligence? We can build upon the search-matching framework, augmented by the assignment model of matching workers' skills and abilities to job tasks, to understand what these new challenges mean

---

[1]By technological diffusion from the frontier economies, we mean the use of capital goods, and local production of goods, that were previously developed by the technology leaders such as the G7 countries. By indigenous innovation, we mean the local development of new product varieties, higher-quality products than currently available in the market, and new production processes.

for the unemployment rate, wage earnings, and income inequalities.[2] I identify boosting the supply of innovators and facilitating the assortative matching of workers' skills to new job tasks as central elements of the strategy needed to keep the unemployment rate low and to generate growth in wage earnings, allowing the standard of living to grow.

New Challenges

The period of growth in Singapore's first 50 years of economic development was mainly fueled by technological diffusion from the frontier economies. The economy achieved its take-off by building a system of secure property rights, a generally business-friendly environment, and a stable industrial relations climate that encouraged a deep integration into the global economy. This combination of institution-building features enabled technology transfer from the frontier economies. One characteristic of such a growth process is that of economic convergence, meaning that the level of technology applied in the Singapore economy grew faster, thus causing the output per worker also to grow faster, the bigger the technology gap. As Singapore's technology gap narrowed, the rate of technological growth invariably declined. While Singapore's continued integration into the global economy will ensure that it continues to benefit from technological developments elsewhere, the impetus for further growth will have to come from indigenous innovation — the local development of new product varieties, higher-quality products, and new production processes.

Suppose that the Singapore economy is on a balanced-growth path where applied technology grows at the rate of 2 percent per annum, mainly fueled by indigenous innovation. To achieve a steady growth of real wages without causing a steady rise in unemployment, it is

---

[2]A pioneering paper that developed the assignment model is Andrew D. Roy, 1951, "Some Thoughts on the Distribution of Earnings," *Oxford Economic Papers*, 3(2): 135–146. A useful survey paper is Michael Sattinger, 1993, "Assignment Models of the Distribution of Earnings," *Journal of Economic Literature* 31(2): 831–880.

not enough that a fixed number of innovative ideas be produced each year. A simple calculation suggests why this is so. Suppose that the current stock of ideas already discovered and in use in Singapore is 1,000. Let the number of new ideas created each year in Singapore be 20. The first year, the growth rate of ideas is equal to 2 percent. In the second year, the growth rate of ideas is 1.96 percent. The growth rate in subsequent years will be 1.92 percent, 1.89 percent, 1.85 percent, 1.82 percent, etc. In order to achieve a constant growth rate of innovative ideas, the number of ideas must grow at a compound rate. Only then can total factor productivity grow at 2 percent to match wage expectations without causing the unemployment rate to rise.[3] An important question is: What will produce a steady flow of indigenous innovations that will deliver this 2 percent growth in ideas for new and higher-quality products? A line of research on economic growth has emphasised the role played by people in generating innovative ideas.[4]

Making the Transition to Indigenous Innovation

The first challenge ahead of us is whether we can successfully transit from growth based on technological diffusion from frontier economies to generating indigenous innovation. It is helpful in facing this challenge to note that, even within an industry, there is a whole distribution of firms based on their productivity level and their size. Consequently, there is scope to generate technological diffusion from the more productive firms to the less productive ones within the local economy. The large and productive firms tend to be export-oriented and adopt good management practices. To deliver innovative products, each small and medium-sized firm might not benefit so much from knowledge developed by firms operating at the world's

---

[3]Total factor productivity growth is the growth of total GDP that remains after subtracting the growth of factor inputs. The creation of new product varieties and higher-quality products contribute to growth in total factor productivity.

[4]An early reference is Edmund S. Phelps, 1968, "Population increase," *Canadian Journal of Economics*, 1(3): 497–518. A later reference is Charles I. Jones, 2005, "Growth and Ideas," in *Handbook of Economic Growth*, Volume 1A, Philippe Aghion and Steven Durlauf (eds.), Amsterdam: Elsevier.

technology frontier but from more productive firms based locally instead. Learning from locally-based firms and building on their ideas might provide the needed impetus to launch a slightly differentiated product variety or better-quality product. With a culture being developed to encourage business innovation from early on in the education system, working first in a multinational corporation to learn good management practices before launching a startup will help to increase the supply of new products. In the presence of Marshallian externalities, there is also a role for government support at the sectoral level to teach better management practices, for example, and to lower the fixed cost of selling into export markets. When more productive firms sell into the international market, the process of exporting itself sometimes teaches the firms' employees to tackle new problems not faced before. In the process of learning to solve new problems, they grow to become even more productive. This widens the local technology gap for the less productive firms, enhancing local technological diffusion and indigenous innovation, which provides a new source of growth. In the food and beverage business, local firms currently selling only within Singapore can learn from those who have successfully entered the regional market.

Coping with a Shrinking Workforce

The second challenge comes from the projected decline in the size of the local workforce, given past total fertility rates. In the basic neoclassical growth model developed by the economist Robert Solow, where technological progress is exogenous, a decline in the size of the labour force actually raises the amount of physical capital per worker and boosts the standard of living.[5] However, if technological progress is the result of innovative ideas being created by people, and thus is endogenous, then there is a concern that a decline in the size of the workforce leads to a decline in the growth of innovative ideas. There is some scope for boosting the supply of innovators coming

---

[5]Robert M. Solow, 1956, "A Contribution to the Theory of Economic Growth," *Quarterly Journal of Economics*, 70(1): 65–94.

from creating a whole new culture of risk-taking and launching novel business ideas. Facilitating human interactions so that people learn from others also helps to make up to some extent for having fewer people. Nevertheless, it would appear to be the case that as the population ages without a steady flow of young people entering the economy, the supply of innovators is likely to shrink. In turn, this would cause a growth slowdown. A recent paper used predicted variation in the rate of population ageing across U.S. states over the period 1980–2010 to estimate the economic impact of ageing on state GDP per capita.[6] The paper found that a 10 percent increase in the fraction of the population aged 60 and above decreased the growth rate of state GDP per capita by 5.5 percent. It attributed two-thirds of the reduction in state GDP per capita to slower growth in the labour productivity of workers *across the age distribution*, which includes younger workers. The authors interpret this finding as an indication that older and younger workers are complements in production so the productivity of the older workforce affects the productivity of younger workers. They also suggest that the amount of positive spillovers of older workers on younger workers is reduced if productive older workers are more likely to exit the labour force.[7] In Singapore, the effort to help older workers remain active in the workforce will help to attenuate this. Another hypothesis, which the authors do not examine, is that there are fewer new business ventures launched in states that have an older age structure. Future research can test whether this hypothesis holds as it has policy implications for Singapore as it develops indigenous innovation.

Shifting Job Preferences

The third challenge comes from the fact that as the standard of living and wealth increase, and educational attainments are higher,

---

[6]Nicole Maestas, Kathleen J. Mullen, and David Powell, 2016, "The Effect of Population Aging on Economic Growth, the Labor Force and Productivity," NBER Working Paper No. 22452. The paper used the predetermined component of a state's age structure, namely its age structure 10 years prior, as an instrumental variable for its changing age structure.

[7]See Maestas et al. (2016), p. 31.

workers' job preferences shift. There are job tasks that people willingly performed when they were poor but would shun when they are richer. A person with a degree in engineering might, for example, prefer to work in the financial sector. An implication of this is that the goods and services produced by performing these job tasks would become relatively more expensive. The rise in the relative price would indirectly boost the pay that firms are willing to offer thus attracting some workers who previously shunned these job tasks at the previous pay scale. An important idea from the assignment model of matching workers' skills and abilities to job tasks is that a competitive labour market leads workers with different skill levels to be matched with job tasks of different complexities based upon comparative advantage. Suppose also that comparative advantage is positively associated with absolute advantage so that a high-skill person is not only relatively, but also in absolute terms, more productive than a low-skill person in solving complex business problems. Such a competitive equilibrium is socially efficient. However, suppose that workers' job preferences shift for reasons unrelated to comparative advantage so that, say, a job in the financial services sector becomes more attractive than a job in the manufacturing sector. Then the size of the economy's total GDP will be sub-optimal (that is, below the socially efficient level) as people without comparative advantage choose to work in the financial services sector. The employment share of the manufacturing sector will be sub-optimally low while the employment share of the financial services sector will be sub-optimally large. Possibly, providing better information about the nature of work in different industries will help to facilitate the assortative matching between workers' skills and job tasks to achieve social optimum.

Facing Technological Disruptions

The fourth challenge comes from automation, robotisation and artificial intelligence, which can transform many work processes, making certain occupations specialising in routine tasks such as bill processing, data entry, and repetitive assembly line production less in demand. There are, however, many other tasks that are not so easy to automate such as helping to clean up a bed-ridden patient, discussing business strategies, and managing inter-personal relationships at the workplace. In the U.S. and Euro zone countries, where this process appears to have been at work for at least the past decade and a half, this has led to a polarisation of the labour market. If middle-skilled jobs are replaced, there must inevitably be a reallocation of labour towards jobs at the low and high ends of the pay scale. Jobs at the high end of the pay scale very likely require a university degree but jobs at the low end do not require high academic qualifications. If there is any reluctance on the part of Singaporeans to take up jobs at the low end of the pay scale, employers will exert a disproportionately large demand for low-wage foreign workers to fill these jobs. Since middle-wage jobs are generally on the decline due to automation and artificial intelligence, and not all Singaporeans will be able to secure a high-paying job, the fact that recessions tend to have a disproportionate impact on young workers lacking certified skills might force many among the next generation of young people to take up these low-wage jobs. It is not implausible that, in a decade or two, the minimum age eligibility (currently at 35 years old) for wage income supplements to low-wage workers might have to be lowered. Subsidies to retrain middle-wage workers will equip them with new skills that can be matched to more complex job tasks. Jobs will also have to be restructured. This will help more workers to qualify for jobs at the higher end of the pay scale. While advances in robotics and artificial intelligence produce robots that substitute for certain tasks previously performed by humans, there are also multiplicative robots that boost the productivity of workers. There is also a silver lining in this for workers.

Some Lessons

What lessons are there to draw on how Singapore ought to face its new challenges by examining how the country tackled the four challenges in the past half century? The first lesson is that choosing to remain integrated into the global economy enabled the country to ride on waves of opportunities that the world economy and technology brought. Even as the economy transits from technological diffusion from frontier economies to indigenous innovation, selling into the global economy still remains a vital element of the strategy to generate good jobs. As the frontier economies appear to enter into a period of slower growth, and there are threats of trade wars, the development of the regional economies provides a market for new businesses to sell into and invest in.

The second lesson is that successful matching of workers with the right skills to meet the needs of the new jobs will help to keep the unemployment rate low. Our schools can seek to teach people how to learn, and to adapt to learn things through life, so that they can thrive in an environment fraught with novelties. In addition, while it is the private business enterprises that will create most of the new jobs, the government can facilitate a close communication between businesses and training institutions so that supply can match the demand for new skills.

The third lesson is that a good supply of innovators is needed to launch new business ventures and become productive to sell into the world market. Invariably, this will mean facing adverse external shocks. In order to finance jobs credits during episodes of negative external shocks, the government would need to save during good times. Even though the phase of catch-up growth is over, mature economies sometimes face prolonged periods when economic activity picks up such as during the U.S. internet boom in the late nineties. During such booms, tax revenues increase (at given tax rates). A fiscally prudent government will save up these additional fiscal resources in order to use them to hasten economic recoveries when negative shocks hit the economy.

The fourth lesson is that an economy exhibiting economic dynamism expands the tax base on a sustained basis thus enabling the government to have the fiscal resources to fund wage income supplements for low-skill workers as well as employment and training subsidies for middle-skill workers. The optimal tax structure reflects higher tax burdens on those highly rewarded by the market to help finance subsidies to those at the lower end of the before-tax income distribution.

Chapter 11

The Good Economy and the Good Life

It is evident that we don't each live alone on an island, like Robinson Crusoe.[1] Instead, we live within a *society* with other people within a particular geographical area. There are rights and obligations as members of that society, typically organised with a government that has a monopoly on violence. From the perspective of a good economy, the important feature of a society is that collaboration among the citizens, each with different abilities (both innate and acquired), in production and exchange according to the principle of comparative advantage results in a social surplus. In other words, the total output produced by all the workers with differing skill levels from social collaboration is greater than the sum of the outputs of individuals working alone. The gains from international trade between one country and the rest of the world can further expand this social surplus.

The nature of the social collaboration changes as an economy grows. Yet, that growth is never assured since the future is fraught with uncertainty. In the process of generating growth, the element of hope keeps a society's citizens going even as the going gets tough. A lot of self-discovery forms part of what we might call a good life even when the citizens start off being rather poor. Discovery takes a new form when citizens start off life with greater wealth. We also find

---

[1]See Daniel Defoe, 2003 [originally published in 1719], *Robinson Crusoe*, New York: Barnes and Noble Classics.

that our discovery often depends on our interactions and feedback we receive from others so maintaining good human relationships is part of the good life. As the fruit of social collaboration is not equal across all citizens in a free market economy, a concept of economic justice that gives weight to the wellbeing of the disadvantaged workers should guide our policymaking.

Social Collaboration and Social Surplus

Suppose that there are two types of jobs, where a job can be defined in terms of the relative importance of two different tasks: problem-solving and manual dexterity. The job that is relatively more intensive in problem-solving produces good X while the job that is relatively more intensive in manual dexterity produces good Y. There are two types of workers: one type is relatively better at performing the job intensive in problem-solving while the other type is relatively better at performing the job intensive in manual dexterity. Let's say that all workers prefer to consume some of each good. Without social collaboration, every worker would devote his time to performing both jobs. However, the economy's output would be greater if each worker specialises in one job according to his comparative advantage. The total output produced in an economy with social collaboration would exceed the sum of the individual outputs produced when every worker did both jobs. That difference is the social surplus.

Our skill level is in part innate. On the other hand, there are important skills that we can acquire through training. In a market economy, firms advertise job vacancies while workers search for good job matches. An economy that does a better job of facilitating the matching of workers to jobs based on their comparative advantage enjoys a greater social surplus. The size of the social surplus can also be increased from engaging with the global economy. When an economy is initially far away from the technology frontier, the ability to create the right social infrastructure to facilitate technology transfer ensures that the size of the social surplus grows at a very rapid pace. As a mature economy, it will be the ability to organise society to stimulate a fast pace of innovation that would cause the social surplus to expand.

What can cause the social surplus to shrink? This can come about when groups form to block the mechanisms for maximising the social surplus. The misallocation of resources can also stymie the growth of social surplus. Having increased our standard of living over the past five decades, what can cause our living standard to actually decline? It is unlikely that technology will suffer a major decline causing output per head to collapse. We have observed that advanced industrial economies that suffer a sharp fall in capital stock per worker, such as during earthquakes, make rapid recoveries as the economies rebuild the destroyed capital stock with high investments. Having increased the average educational attainment of its citizens, it is unlikely that future workers will have lower levels of human capital. It is more likely that a reversal in fortunes, if it occurs, will come from a failure of a society to hold together through collaboration among its citizens. Preserving that social collaboration and becoming willing to share the economic gains more broadly across the income distribution through the tax-subsidy system will be vital to maintain economic prosperity in the next phase of Singapore's economic development.

Hope

Looking back, there is evidence that our choice to be integrated with the global economy through encouraging the inflow of foreign direct investment facilitated the transfer of technology. The multinational corporations brought into our shores the technology developed originally in the frontier economies. Our ready-to-learn and disciplined workforce facilitated the application of the technology on the production floor to produce goods that were exported. Not all the parts and components used in the production process were produced locally. Many of them were simply imported from abroad. Through these mechanisms, the technology gap steadily narrowed. However, for the citizens of Singapore in the 1960s, none of the positive pull on wages and employment was assured. The results to the participants in the early decades of our economic development were uncertain. In such an environment, it must be the hope that life would indeed get better that propelled the workers to give their best to the job responsibilities. The element of hope must also have positive spillovers on the children of the workers who could spend more time to acquire the education that their parents did not have. That sense of optimism was contagious, enabling the country to resolve conflicts such as fighting the 1985 recession via cost cutting achieved by reducing the CPF contribution rate of employers.

In the next phase of growth, it is giving this sense of hope — that Singapore will succeed in transforming the small and medium-sized enterprises into productive firms that can break into overseas markets — that will inspire a steady stream of innovators. Just as the pioneer generation started with a low living standard and came to imagine a future with good jobs and good pay, so also can their children and grandchildren make a transition from being a technology follower to becoming an economy capable of doing indigenous innovation.

Discovery

Much of our investments require looking far ahead to reap the rewards. The investment made by an entrepreneur to start a business involves incurring a current cost to enjoy a stream of expected future profits. An innovator who chooses not to take on a paid job but devotes the time to come out with a better-quality intermediate input looks forward to displacing a current product with another and thus earn a stream of profits before being overtaken by another rival. An individual who decides to spend another year to further his education rather than to work looks forward to enjoying higher pay in a job with new responsibilities. Because the future is unknown, each investment that is made is an expression of hope. However, there is also another element that is part of a good life, which is the discovery.

In part, this discovery is of something about oneself that is not known before one makes the investment commitment. Another part is the discovery of new things that one did not know before. The entrepreneur learns about the market that he is trying to sell his products into. The market research that is done to discern customers' taste and implementing sales strategies to expand market share all form part of a discovery process. One also gets to discover whether one has the strengths to succeed as an entrepreneur. The investment to increase human capital enables one to start a learning journey. Later, the integration of what one has learnt in class to the workplace also enhances the joy of discovery.

Human Relationships

One never learns in isolation. A part of what we learn about ourselves and about our world comes from human interactions. The ability to relate to others and learn from others — those who are our peers, those whom we supervise, and those we report to in our work — is a vital part of our being well-functioning individuals in a society. Many projects that are undertaken at the modern workplace require team effort. A dynamic economy provides the impetus for people to face new challenges, which draws them together in collaboration. That learning, in fact, begins much earlier when we are still children. We learn from our parents and siblings at home, which helps us develop both cognitive and non-cognitive skills that make us effective workers when we grow up. At school, we also learn from our schoolmates. A good economy is one that will devote resources to ensuring that children from disadvantaged families do not miss out on opportunities to learn from others.

A part of the joy we derive from living a good life comes from fulfilling a sense of responsibility in the different roles we play in society — as employees, as citizens, as members of social groups, as siblings, as sons or daughters, and as spouses. When we act responsibly in our different roles, we get a sense of satisfaction. A worker who does his job conscientiously and with an attitude of excellence even when nobody else sees him doing it derives intrinsic joy. It is striking how despite the ten-fold increase in standard of living Singapore has enjoyed over the past 50 years, the sense of collegiality enjoyed with colleagues over a cup of coffee and cake today is not very different from the past.

Economic Justice

Any nation, in order to enjoy economic prosperity — which gives its citizens the joy of living, the thrill of meeting challenges, and the financial resources to help the economically disadvantaged — must generate economic dynamism which comes from riding the waves of opportunities that the global economy throws up. Singapore embraced this economic openness in its past nearly half century and has enjoyed the fruits of that integration. It must now find the means to gear its political and economic institutions to continue to embrace economic openness in facing the next half century to deliver good jobs and wages. As the philosopher John Rawls argued:

> [S]o long as we believe for good reasons that a self-sustaining and reasonably just political and social order both at home and abroad is possible, we can reasonably hope that we or others will someday, somewhere, achieve it; and we can then do something toward this achievement. This alone, quite apart from our success or failure, suffices to banish the dangers of resignation and cynicism.[2]

And so in embracing economic openness to have the good life, we also need to continue to embrace the economically disadvantaged and aid them in this process. Together, then, Singapore can truly outshine its past and create something that is viable and miraculously possible, giving its citizens a truly good life.

---

[2]See John Rawls, 1999, *The Law of Peoples*, Cambridge, MA: Harvard University Press, p. 128.

Epilogue

What does it take for an economy whose standard of living places it among the rich countries in the world to stagnate and fall behind? Natural disasters such as earthquakes and events like wars can cause a sudden drop in living standards when capital stocks are destroyed, leaving surviving workers with less machines to work with. Experiences of countries, however, have shown that, with institutions left intact, high rates of investment motivated by high rates of return to capital following these episodes bring about fast recoveries. In fact, the new machines put in place might incorporate new technologies thus boosting productivity per worker. What is more likely to cause a rich economy to fall behind is a breakdown in its political institutions brought about by a loss of social and economic inclusion.

Market forces acted to foster economic inclusion before the turn of the new millennium as comparative advantage in less skill-intensive goods led to an increase in the earnings of the less skilled workers relative to the more skilled. Since about the year 2000, shifts in comparative advantage towards more skill-intensive goods and the onslaught of skill-biased technology have led to a widening of the wage gap. To maintain economic inclusion now requires national wage supplement schemes to boost the earnings of low-wage workers. Current and future workers also face the advances of artificial intelligence and machine learning that will destroy jobs that involve routine tasks, but also create new opportunities from the increased labour demand for workers in jobs requiring non-routine tasks, inter-personal communications, and face-to-face contact. The pay structure that will adjust to reflect increased labour demand for non-routine tasks and decreased demand for routine tasks is likely to worsen wage inequality.

The optimal form of social safety nets to provide, and the best way to use limited funds to help improve economic and social outcomes of the disadvantaged, will have to be determined without the tailwind of catch-up growth. Allocating funds to achieve the highest social returns to improving adult economic outcomes would need to recognise that both cognitive as well as non-cognitive skills (such as having motivation and perseverance, and being able to get along with others) at a very young age are important predictors of adult success. Research findings provide evidence that the performance of adults in the workplace, which is correlated with their employability, pay, and job satisfaction, is strongly determined by both cognitive and non-cognitive skills acquired when they were relatively young.[1] While job retraining for the current pool of older workers, who missed out on the opportunity to pursue higher education when Singapore began its modern growth, must continue apace, the aforementioned research findings carry important implications for parents, educators, and policy makers as we look ahead to the next few decades.

Because of the forces tending to widen income inequalities and limit social mobility, Singapore will continue to have disadvantaged families and workers even as it matures and joins the ranks of developed economies. Even as more pathways are opened for an increased intake of students into higher educational institutions, there has to be an investment to improve the life outcomes of citizens coming from disadvantaged families. It appears that government funds fetch the highest social returns when invested in young people beginning from pre-school levels. Because non-cognitive skills are found to be so important in shaping adult performance at work, and they can be shaped by early interventions, it is necessary to bring

---

[1]See James Heckman, 2008, "Schools, Skills, and Synapses," *Economic Inquiry*, 46(3): 289–324. Professor Heckman provides an overview of the research findings about the importance of non-cognitive skills (on top of cognitive skills) acquired when young for positive adult economic outcomes.

parents on board in programmes using public funds to help build the self-esteem, motivation, and perseverance of disadvantaged young people. Charitable non-governmental organisations with an interest to engage young people also play a vital role in strengthening the ability of young people to pursue worthwhile goals. Such skills learnt at a young age generate great pay-offs when they become adults.

Going forward, with a fertility rate that is below replacement level, having no net immigration will mean an actual decline of Singapore's total population. Combined with longer life expectancy, this will mean a higher dependency ratio as well as a larger share of older workers in the total workforce. It would seem necessary to augment the local workforce with some level of net immigration of younger workers to avoid a future fiscal crunch. The steady inflow of foreign direct investment can potentially support new jobs for both local and foreign workers without depressing wages since the multinational firms also invest in physical capital and new technology, which will act to boost labour productivity and pay. There will, however, be increased pressure on our limited land. The inflow of foreign workers provides both gains and costs to the citizenry that they will have to apportion in a rational benefit-cost analysis. There would also have to be an investment in building social cohesion within a more heterogeneous population.

Index